Reignite

A Guide to Overcoming Burnout

Dr. Suzanne Alari

Table of Contents

Introduction

We live in a world of high expectations placed on us by ourselves, our family and peers, and our society. Most of us have too much to do and too little time to do it. And, with technology, especially smartphones, so integrated into our everyday lives, switching off has become nearly impossible. How often do you sit at the dinner table, in front of the television, or getting ready for bed when a work email comes through, and you think: "This will only take a second. It could be important. I've been waiting for this response all day." This situation likely happens more often than you would care to admit, and it's a terrible problem society is facing—the inability to switch off from work.

And although it is seemingly a part of "normal life" because everyone does it, there is nothing normal about being in a work-space mind frame 24 hours a day, seven days a week. Nothing! The results of this mind frame are visible in every sector of our lives. They affect our family, friends, mental health, and overall satisfaction. Moreover, being in a constant work-space mind frame reduces your productivity and can lead to a severe health condition—*burnout*.

The World Health Organization (WHO) defines burnout as "a syndrome conceptualized as resulting from chronic workplace stress that has not been successfully managed. It is characterized by three dimensions: feelings of energy depletion or exhaustion; increased mental distance from one's job, or feelings of negativism or cynicism related to one's job; and reduced professional efficacy" (World Health Organization, 2019).

Burnout is a condition that hasn't really been discussed until recently. While people have always risked being burned out at work, it has become more common over the past five years, especially during and after the pandemic—a global event that irreversibly changed countless lives. Many people don't consider burnout to be a real problem. They think that if they focus a little more on sleep, healthy eating, or exercise, they will start to feel better, and their symptoms will disappear. Unfortunately, this isn't the case. Yes, healthy lifestyle changes can reduce the effects of burnout and stress. But if you don't make proactive changes in your work life and schedule, you will never truly overcome the burnout monster.

Of course, it's easy for me to say that you should reorganize your schedule to overcome and prevent burnout. It's much harder to actually put this advice to use, especially during crunch times at work, which seem to be all the time nowadays. Understanding exactly what burnout is and which steps you can take to overcome your burnout and prevent it from happening again should be a priority. Whether you are an employee, a team leader, or an employer, understanding the signs and effects of burnout will help you identify and treat it much more effectively.

I have worked in the medical industry for more than 20 years, and I have seen firsthand how damaging burnout can be. I have suffered from severe burnout myself and have had to work extremely hard to overcome it to prevent it from happening again. As a result, I have learned many coping skills and effective ways to reduce, prevent, and treat burnout. I have also treated many patients who suffer from burnout and have seen what catastrophic effects burnout has had in their lives. I've spent years developing a successful treatment plan for burnout, and I now wish to share that knowledge with you.

A quick search on the internet will supply you with many tips and tricks for reducing and preventing burnout. However, these tips often don't target the root cause of your burnout. Instead, they often merely offer you some advice for better coping with the problem.

I don't believe this is enough. Burnout has catastrophic effects, not only on your mental health but also on your physical health and emotional well-being. Experiencing severe stress for extended periods puts your body in survival mode. Your adrenaline levels are increased, you sleep less, and your body is in a constant fight-or-flight state. Being under a severe amount of stress leads to various health problems, including compromised immunity, insomnia, and depression. As such, it is not merely enough to learn how to manage your burnout.

Unfortunately, no. What is required is a treatment plan for curing your current burnout and an active plan for preventing it from returning.

That is what this book offers. If you are tired of feeling drained and powerless, of not being able to switch off and connect with those around you, or constantly waiting for the other shoe to drop, then this is the book for you. In this book, you will learn everything there is to know about burnout and how to overcome it. Some topics covered in this book include:

- Identifying the signs of burnout.

- Identifying the cause of burnout.

- The effects of burnout on yourself and others.

- Overcoming burnout.

- Preventing burnout from returning.

This book will also discuss how men and women experience and treat burnout differently. Men and women also process stress differently. Their unique roles within a family structure also mean that their responsibilities outside of work are different, which also affects how they experience and handle stress. You will learn what role a team leader or employer plays in identifying and preventing burnout. You will also discover why conventional solutions for dealing with burnout aren't effective. There are many suggestions for treating burnout, but they don't offer a real solution.

In this world of "always on, always available," it can seem impossible to take the time to switch off from work and make your health (mental and physical) a priority. But what is the point of working yourself to the bone for 40 years if you won't have the health to enjoy retirement? What's the point of working yourself into a stupor, of making enough money to enjoy life's luxuries if you don't have the time or energy to do so? We are supposed to work so we can live. But recently, it has become more of a situation where we are surviving to work. Few people have a healthy work-life balance, and even fewer can say that their mental health is a priority and is in good standing. But all that is about to change. It has to be for your health and the health and happiness of those around you. With that in mind, let's dive into the first chapter, which discusses how to identify burnout in yourself.

Chapter 1:

Do I Suffer From Burnout?

Most people experience stressful times at work or in their personal lives. This makes it difficult for many to determine whether they are experiencing a normal amount of stress or if they are moving into burnout territory. And some people refuse to accept that they are burnt-out, even if they know that they do, in fact, suffer from burnout. Why is this? Well, many people feel that if they ignore the signs of their burnout, they will soon start feeling better again. Others think they simply don't have the time to worry about being burnt-out when there is so much work to be done. And some people merely believe that being stressed is a normal part of life.

And it is, to some extent. Stress is normal, and you will experience times of increased stress at work or in other areas of your life from time to time. But when your stress becomes so much that it starts influencing your mental well-being, physical health, and social relationships, it becomes a problem. And while you may not think that you have to address your stress, you will realize its significant impact when it is too late. When does stress turn into burnout?

Elizabeth Scott at Verywell Mind (2022) states, "Stress turns into burnout when you experience it for too long, or when your stress becomes more than you can handle." Prolonged periods of stress can easily turn into burnout, especially when that stress isn't managed properly. Unfortunately, many people are so used to having constant stress in their work environment that they fail to recognize when their stress is turning into something more.

Therefore, this chapter will focus on helping you determine whether you or your loved one is merely stressed or if you are nearing burnout and need to take a step back and focus on your emotional and mental health. You will learn what burnout looks like, what lifestyle choices increase your chances of burnout, and how your personality affects your chances of experiencing burnout. You will also learn about one test you can take to determine if you are at risk of burning out. But first, what does burnout look like?

What Are the Signs and Symptoms of Burnout?

When it comes to determining whether someone is burnt-out, you may wonder how burnout looks different from stress, if these two states are even distinguishable from each other. While it is difficult to distinguish stress from burnout, slight differences between the two can help you establish which problem you have.

Stress and Burnout

Burnout might be described as an extended period of overwhelming stress, but the condition isn't the same as being stressed. "Some stress, such as stress before a deadline, is good, as it can boost your productivity, energy levels, and alertness" (*Signs You Might,* 2021). This is your body's fight-or-flight response. It can make you faster, stronger, and more alert in times of danger, but even regular stress can become dangerous if you experience it too often or cannot handle it.

Stress affects your sleep, mood, and overall well-being. Studies have shown that increased stress can lead to lower immunity, an increased risk of certain cancers, and increased depression rates. So, no stress is good if you experience it for too long. But, if stress turns to burnout, it is even more dangerous for you and those around you.

Physical Signs of Burnout

Like stress, burnout manifests itself in many different ways. One of the most obvious signs that you are burnt-out is if you experience any of these physical symptoms regularly:

- Extreme fatigue that doesn't improve with sleep. Even if you get eight hours of sleep daily, you wake up exhausted and often need a mid-morning energy boost.

- Digestive issues despite eating the same food you normally do. Bloating, indigestion, and sudden food allergies indicate that your body is experiencing increased amounts of stress.

- Headaches that don't disappear. These headaches often appear despite taking pain medication or return as soon as the medication wears off.

- Frequent illnesses despite normally being a healthy person. If you never get sick and suddenly feel under the weather quite often despite taking your vitamins and eating healthy, it signifies that your body is stressed.

- Insomnia even though you are tired. If you wake up feeling exhausted and still toss and turn all night without proper rest, it is a sign that your brain is overstimulated and that you are suffering from burnout.

- Changes in your appetite—eating either more than you usually do or scarcely eating anything.

These symptoms are similar to those of stress. However, if you notice these symptoms for extended periods, even after the stressful situation, like the deadline, has passed, it could be a sign that you are suffering from burnout.

Behavioral Signs of Burnout

Burnout not only affects your physical well-being but also your emotional health. And this may lead to changes in your behavior, which you wouldn't necessarily expect and are completely opposite to your normal self. Burnout affects every part of your life, not only your work life. Therefore, people may notice changes in your behavior wherever you go. Some behavioral changes that might signify burnout include:

- Using substances like alcohol, drugs, or sugar to cope with your feelings of stress and anxiety.

- Isolating yourself from others, even those who are closest to you, when you are normally a social person.

- Not being as productive as you usually are, even when there are deadlines to meet at work.

- Not being as dedicated as you normally are—coming into work later than normal and leaving earlier.

- Procrastinating instead of getting things done as soon as possible.

- Having a shorter temper than normal, especially when you are known to be patient.

Again, many of these symptoms are similar to those you may experience when you are merely stressed. However, other symptoms, like decreased productivity, are contrary to what most people experience when stressed.

Emotional Signs of Burnout

Because burnout affects your emotional well-being as well as your physical one, you may experience some emotional changes when burnt-out too. It's important that you pay attention to these signs, as burnout may lead to depression or worsened depression if it is something you have struggled with in the past. Isolation is also a symptom and a cause of depression, so the behavioral changes you experience when you feel burnt-out can also cause depression to arise or resurface. Some emotional signs of burnout include:

- Having a negative outlook on life no matter how good your day was. Even if you had a day of resting, spending time with family or friends, or doing what you love, you still feel cynical about everything and see only the downsides.

- Feeling trapped or misunderstood more than you normally do, even when your loved ones try to understand your perspective.

- Having a complete loss of motivation, even when doing things you ordinarily do for fun. Not feeling motivated to pursue your hobbies is a clear sign that your emotional health isn't well.

- Feeling defensive or numb. Burnout can have one of two results. It can either make you feel that everyone is criticizing you, no matter how hard you work or what you do. On the contrary, burnout can also cause you to become emotionally stunted, failing to empathize with those around you or to try to see things from their perspective.

- In addition to seeing only the bad things in life, burnout can also lead to feeling unsatisfied, regardless of your accomplishments. Even when you reach the milestones you have worked so hard toward, burnout can make you feel like you simply aren't good enough.

- Burnout can also make you feel helpless like there is nothing you can do to overcome the challenges you are faced with. It can cause you to feel isolated and powerless.

Considering how serious these physical, behavioral, and emotional symptoms of burnout are and how much damage they can do, it is crucial that you take the right measures to cure your burnout and prevent it from returning. Of course, knowing the symptoms of burnout is but one part of the story. The other part is discovering what has caused it.

Lifestyle Choices and Careers That Predispose One to Burnout

While burnout isn't always the result of your actions, some things you might be doing could be causing you to burn out. Certain lifestyle choices and careers put you at a higher risk for burnout. But it's important to consider that no matter what your career, you can still experience burnout, especially if you have been stressing about work or your personal life for a long time. Your lifestyle often significantly affects your stress and potential burnout more so than your career. So, which lifestyle choices can lead to burnout?

Lifestyle Choices That Affect Burnout

Regardless of your career, certain lifestyle choices make you more prone to burning out, especially when other factors, such as deadlines or cash flow problems, come into play. Many students also face burnout despite not even having a job yet, which further proves that your career doesn't have as much to do with your potential for burnout as certain other factors. *HelpGuide.Org* (Smith et al., 2018) shares five lifestyle choices that increase your risk of burning out.

All Work; No Play

If you are a workaholic, chances are you have already suffered from burnout or are on the straight path to experiencing it eventually. While it's great to have ambitions and goals at work, it's also important to maintain a healthy work-life balance. Unfortunately, if you are constantly working or thinking about work, you don't have a work-life balance. In this case, your mind may become overactive, and you will have trouble sleeping or functioning normally, increasing your chances of burning out.

Too Little Sleep

A lack of sleep has severe consequences for your mental and physical health. It can lead to the development of several health conditions, burnout being one of them. If you are fatigued, your brain won't cope with stress as well as it should. You also won't be able to process your emotions as well as you usually do. As a result, you may start to feel overwhelmed much sooner and suffer from burnout as a result. Of course, too little sleep alone may not cause burnout. But it can increase the effects of other factors, such as stress, on your mental health, leading to burnout.

No Social Interaction or Downtime

A part of being a workaholic is that you don't take time to see your family and friends. You also don't make time for downtime, like pursuing a hobby or catching up on your favorite series. These mundane actions are crucial for improving your mental health and ensuring you are emotionally stable. Pursuing your hobbies and having social interactions help to release your happy hormones and reduce your stress hormones, helping reduce the chances of burnout. So, you are more likely to burn out if you don't have any social interactions or downtime.

Taking on Too Many Responsibilities

Despite being goal-driven, you should know when to draw the line when taking on more responsibilities. For example, if you have children or family to care for, you cannot commit to taking on more work if that interferes with your time caring for them. You will become overwhelmed with work and responsibilities, which may increase your chances of burnout. Ensure your schedule allows for downtime. And if you are already stretched too thin, don't take on more responsibilities.

Not Asking For Help When You Need It

People often feel too proud to ask for help, even when they realize they are overwhelmed. They think asking for help will make them look like a failure, making them weak. Even though most of us know this isn't true, we still tend to feel that way. However, not asking for help when needed is one way to increase your odds of burning out quite significantly. You will soon feel overwhelmed if you don't consult your loved ones or ask them for help when needed. As a result, your odds of burning out will increase even more.

While these lifestyle choices are often to blame for burnout, some careers and professions further increase the risk of burning out simply because of how much strain they cause. So, which careers are more likely to cause burnout, you may ask?

Careers With a Higher Burnout Rate Than Average

Some careers are inherently more stressful than others. For example, we saw during the pandemic what effect additional stress had on healthcare workers and other service providers worldwide. But even if there isn't a pandemic to battle, some careers simply involve more stress than others. Don't misunderstand, though; you can easily burn out in any career if you don't handle stress well. According to one study (Murray, 2022), burnout affects nearly 90% of American adults, regardless of their profession.

But, according to *Slice* magazine (Murray, 2022), the following careers have the highest burnout rates. I've also included the percentage of that workforce who reported burnout in a single year (2021-2022).

- Accountants: 84% reported burnout per year.

- Lawyers: 70% reported burnout per year.

- Emergency response workers: 62% reported burnout per year.

- Retail workers: 58% reported burnout per year.

- Physicians: 53% reported burnout per year.

- Fast food workers: 52% reported burnout per year.

- Teachers: 44% reported burnout per year.

- Air traffic controllers: 40% reported burnout per year.

- Social workers: 39% reported burnout per year.

- Nurses: 25% reported burnout per year.

- Police officers: 15% reported burnout per year.

It's important to consider that this number and these statistics may truly be much higher. Many people who suffer from burnout don't report it, as they either consider their stress a normal part of life or don't want to appear weak by complaining about it to Human Resources (HR). But these statistics are still shocking, even if they don't paint the whole picture. Some consider burnout a global pandemic, a silent killer that nobody talks about and is trying to cure.

How Your Personality Type Affects Your Chances of Burnout

Many studies have researched the link between certain personality traits and burnout. These studies came to some interesting conclusions about why certain people are more likely to experience burnout than others. The correlation between personality and burnout can be disputed. You must consider other factors, such as your career and lifestyle choices, before determining if your personality simply makes you more prone to burning out. That being said, here are five personality traits that put you at a higher risk of burning out.

Type A Personality

Most employers value those with Type A personalities, as they tend to be loyal employees who work harder than most others. However, having a Type A personality also puts you at greater risk of burning out. If you aren't familiar with a Type A personality, *Verywell Mind* (Scott, 2006) describes this personality type as having the following qualities:

- competitive

- fast-paced

- impatient

- goal-orientated

As you can imagine, these are great qualities to have at work. However, they can also make it difficult to accept when you need help or to recognize when you are already too busy. As such, people with Type A personalities are more susceptible to burnout, especially during crunch time at work.

Perfectionism

Being a perfectionist has its perks. But it also has its downfalls. Being a perfectionist is great in a work environment where quality is praised over quantity. However, being a perfectionist in a job with strict deadlines and a lot of external pressure may become overwhelming for a perfectionist. They can easily fall prey to burnout, often struggling to settle for the "done is better than perfect" mentality. Perfectionists don't do well in high-stress environments and may burn out much quicker because of it.

Self-Doubt

Being someone who constantly doubts yourself can also lead to burnout. Self-doubt often leads to higher stress levels and higher perceived levels of stress. Even when other people don't pressure you, you may feel pressured because you don't think you are good enough for the job. A new term called "impostor syndrome" also causes people to experience more stress than they are actually presented with. And because prolonged stress is a leading cause of burnout, people with increased self-doubt are more prone to burnout.

Pessimism

Pessimism isn't a good quality, no matter how you look at it. It causes you to focus solely on the negative aspects of something and disregard the positive events or outcomes. As such, you can imagine that pessimism can easily lead to burnout. Because you are only focused on the negative aspects of something, you are more susceptible to feeling stressed or criticized. This may lead you to focus only on the stress you experience, causing you to become burned out much sooner than someone with a more positive outlook.

Excitability

Another personality trait that can increase your likelihood of suffering from burnout is excitability. Excitability refers to how easily your environment affects your mood. Some people are less excitable than others. They can remain level-headed even under severe pressure or during unpleasant events. On the contrary, other people are more excitable. Their environment greatly affects their mood, both pleasant and unpleasant. They thrive under good circumstances, like office parties or social events. However, they are also easily affected by unpleasant situations, such as tight deadlines or budget cuts. As such, more excitable people are most likely to feel the effects of stress and may become burnt-out much sooner than those who are less excitable.

Of course, if certain personality traits can make you more prone to burning out, others can also make you more resistant to it. In addition, some personality traits make you better equipped to deal with everyday stress, which can also increase your resistance to burnout. Here are five personality traits that may help protect you from burning out.

Self-Confidence

Self-doubt causes increased stress, but self-confidence may actually reduce it. If you are confident in your expertise and skills at work, you are less likely to think you will be on the chopping block should the company downscale. This causes you to feel less stressed or anxious about your work situation, making you more resistant to burnout. If you believe that your work is good enough and that you are doing enough for the company, you won't consider yourself a liability or feel increased stress as much.

Agreeableness

Being an agreeable person (someone who chooses peace over being right), you may find that you also experience less stress. While being agreeable comes with some drawbacks (you are often given more work because you cannot say no), it does mean that you aren't involved in as many conflicts at work, which may also lead to additional stress and an increased risk of burnout. So, while you should manage your agreeableness and not let others take advantage of it, you may also learn that being agreeable reduces your stress which helps prevent burnout.

Openness

Being open is difficult today, as many consider vulnerability a weakness. However, if you are more open and honest about your feelings, you will let other people see when you feel overwhelmed, and they can take some of the burden off your shoulders. This can also help reduce your chances of burnout, as you won't feel as overwhelmed or burdened. Therefore, being open and willing to share your emotions—good and bad—can prevent burnout to some extent.

Extroversion

Being extroverted or introverted is rarely a choice. Either you are one, or you aren't. However, studies have shown that extroverted people tend to have a decreased risk of burnout because they also tend to be more open about their feelings (Angelini, 2023). As an introvert, you may feel uncomfortable sharing your feelings with others. But as an extrovert, you should have less trouble telling others exactly what you think and how you feel about a situation. This can help reduce your burden and reduce the chances of burnout.

Conscientiousness

Angelini (2023) describes conscientiousness as "a personality trait reflected in precise, organized, and disciplined individuals who respect the rules and work hard to achieve success." Their personalities are such that they don't feel the effects of stress as often. Because they are such meticulous planners, they often account for deadlines or other stressors and deal with them as they arise. As such, if you are conscientious, you likely won't experience stress as strongly as others, reducing your chances of burning out.

Using the Burnout Self-Test to See if You Suffer From Burnout

Despite all you have read about burnout and which personality traits, careers, and lifestyle choices are more likely to lead you to suffer burnout, you may still wonder if you are burnt-out or not. Fortunately, there is a self-test you can conduct to see whether you are burnt-out or at risk of burning out. The Maslach Burnout Inventory, or MBI, is a series of questions you can use to determine if you are burnt-out (*Burnout Self-Test*, n.d.). The test consists of three sections: burnout, depersonalization, and personal achievement. For each section, you select which part resonates most with you (from never to every day).

Based on your answers, you can then determine if you are currently burnt-out, if you are likely to suffer from burnout in the future, or if you are merely going through a stressful situation and will feel better once this time has passed. Before considering what has caused your burnout and how you can cure and prevent it, you must first establish whether you suffer from burnout. You can find the Maslach Burnout Inventory self-test in the appendix section of this book. I recommend taking the test before continuing on to the next chapters, as it will give you a better idea of your risk for burnout and can help you determine your next steps.

Key Takeaways From Chapter 1:

- Burnout can be difficult to distinguish from regular stress. But certain physical, behavioral, and emotional symptoms can help you determine if you suffer from burnout.

- Some lifestyle choices, such as taking on too much work and not giving yourself enough downtime, along with certain careers, increase the risk of suffering from burnout. While some careers are more prone to cause burnout, your personality and lifestyle choices play a much bigger role in your likelihood of burning out.

- Certain personality types, such as perfectionism, pessimism, and self-doubt, increase the chances of burning out. On the contrary, other personality traits, like agreeableness, conscientiousness, and self-confidence, decrease your chances of burnout.

- Taking a Maslach Burnout Inventory self-test can help determine if you suffer from burnout.

Now that you have determined whether you are at risk for burning out or are currently burnt-out, you can start to consider what has caused the burnout and how you can cure and prevent it. In the following chapter, you will learn about the possible causes of burnout that may have led to your condition.

Chapter 2:

How Did I Get It? How Did It

Happen to Me?

If you notice that you suffer from burnout, or your BMI test has revealed that you do, you may ponder how it could have happened to you. If you consider yourself someone who deals well with stress, it might be shocking to learn that you may suffer from burnout. And considering how serious burnout is, based on what you have learned in the previous chapter, it should be one of your biggest priorities to overcome burnout and prevent it from happening again. But before you can do this, you must first discover the source of your burnout. What causes burnout, and how did you fall prey to it?

In this chapter, you will learn about the link between burnout, multitasking, and competing priorities. You will also learn about the effects of the COVID-19 pandemic on burnout statistics, a factor that particularly affects those now working from home. Then, you will discover why the conventional treatments for burnout aren't effective in preventing or curing the condition. Finally, you will uncover a practical plan for overcoming burnout. If you suspect you suffer from burnout, now is the time to pay attention. Not treating the condition can lead to severe health conditions, both mentally and physically, and it's essential to get it under control as soon as possible.

So, let's begin by considering potential causes of burnout, specifically relating to balancing your work and personal life.

The Link Between Competing Priorities, Multitasking, and Burnout

Because burnout is related to stress or is caused by prolonged periods of excessive stress, one must consider where this stress comes from. While burnout can result from only one stressor, such as a highly stressful job, that isn't always the case. More often than not, burnout is caused by various factors, including stress from multiple sources. Unfortunately, your personal life isn't always free of stress, and things aren't always perfect outside of work. When this happens, you may experience overwhelming stress, especially if you cannot get around to doing everything that is expected of you.

As is often the case, you may try to juggle everything on your plate. But research indicates that this isn't a useful or sustainable approach (Comer, 2022). While you may feel that you are working yourself to the bone to get around to everything, you are actually being less productive overall than you would be when focusing on an individual assignment. And this may also lead to burnout. Having too many competing priorities and trying to multitask by doing multiple tasks at the same time can also lead to burnout. How is this possible?

How Competing Priorities Affect Burnout

If you have a demanding work life and changes in your personal life also add stress, you may become burned out easily. For example, if you get a promotion at work that adds more stress, and your family dynamic changes (you have a child, your parents move in with you, etc.), you may suddenly experience more stress than you can handle. This is because you now have competing priorities. You are expected to be an efficient and valuable employee, but you are also expected to be there for your family.

Competing priorities don't necessarily happen because of a family dynamic or personal life change. Most people feel that their priorities compete regularly. There is so much pressure to do well at work or with your studies, have a social life, eat healthily, work out, and have the time to take care of yourself and have me-time. But where should you fit all this in? There are only so many hours in a day, and people often feel like they are not getting around to doing everything.

Having competing priorities, which most of us do almost daily, makes prioritizing your health and well-being difficult. This can lead to feeling overwhelmed, making you vulnerable to burnout. But what can you do? Ben Brealy from *Thoughtful Leader* (2020) recommends the following actions when you feel like your competing priorities are causing you to burn out:

- Ask for help.

- Critically examine any deadlines and prioritize your work around them.

- Say no when approached with more responsibilities or time-consuming efforts.

- Drop some of your responsibilities when you have tried the above tips and are still too overwhelmed.

While this advice may be helpful in some circumstances, I strongly feel it doesn't solve your problem. For example, when all your competing priorities are equally important, and you cannot really put any of them on the back burner, these tips won't help you prevent or overcome burnout in the slightest. So, you might consider another approach—multitasking.

How Multitasking Affects Burnout

People have been trying to convince themselves that they are good at multitasking for years. If you complain about having too much to do and too little time to do it, people will often tell you to find a way to multitask, to do multiple things at once. This is a common approach people take to try and get through all of their tasks in a day. But how well does multitasking work? And can multitasking lead to burnout?

According to *Psychology Today* (Comer, 2022), the ability to multitask is a fallacy we have led ourselves and others to believe in for far too long. The brain cannot process multiple pieces of information simultaneously, and doing so leads to cognitive stress and memory processing problems. This, in turn, not only causes you to feel overwhelmed but also affects the quality of your work and overall productivity.

Psychology Today explains that "Multitasking lowers productivity, slows task completion, decreases task quality, creates stress, and leads to burnout" (Comer, 2022) and that we are not built for multitasking, nor has evolution allowed for it. So, instead of helping you get through more tasks at once, multitasking actually increases your stress levels and mental capacity while decreasing the quality of your work and overall productivity. Of course, the increased stress you experience when multitasking may also lead to burnout, especially when you try to multitask for an extended period.

The Effect of the COVID-19 Pandemic on Burnout Statistics

One cannot witness the national burnout statistics without wondering about the effect of the COVID-19 pandemic on these statistics. Since the start of the pandemic in 2020, we have seen a global increase in chronic stress. People stress more about their physical health, their income, and the future of their children and loved ones than ever before. And even though the pandemic has now been contained and things are somewhat "back to normal," the effects of the pandemic still linger in our everyday lives. Few people have recovered from the chronic stress they experienced during the pandemic. Moreover, many are still in the same situation they were in when the pandemic first started.

Most people started working from home during the pandemic, especially when the country was locked down, and movement was restricted. While this was meant to be a temporary solution, several companies realized that working from home decreases the cost to the company and isn't nearly as unproductive as they initially thought. Now, three years after the pandemic's start, many people still work from home—full-time or part-time. And while there are some advantages of a fully remote or hybrid system, employers seem to ignore the cons of this system.

Working from home often comes with more challenges, particularly as you no longer have a dedicated workplace. Even if you have an office space, you often find yourself in it far more than you would if you were at an office. You are more inclined to follow certain working times when working in another location. When you leave the office, you are more inclined to leave your work behind for the day. But this is not true when working from home.

Working from home makes it difficult to switch off from work, as your work is constantly in front of you. How often have you received a work-related phone call or email outside of traditional working hours and tended to it because your workspace is close by? Working from home makes it increasingly difficult to shut off from work, making it more difficult to fully emerge in your other responsibilities, such as family life and social obligations. Not to mention it makes "me time" almost impossible.

Furthermore, working from home further complicates your competing priorities, as you are often forced to multitask by caring for your family and working at the same time. And, as you already know, these factors increase your risk of suffering from burnout. But the pandemic has not only affected those working from home. Studies show that burnout and depression statistics have increased since the start of the pandemic (Lluch-Sanz et al., 2022). And many researchers have concluded that one of the primary causes of burnout due to the pandemic is increased isolation.

Many people were isolated from their loved ones during the pandemic, which caused them to feel neglected, lonely, and forgotten. Furthermore, the strain placed on families where loved ones passed from the pandemic was further increased if you could not say goodbye to your loved one because you were isolated from them. Anyone who had to go to a hospital or healthcare facility in 2020 and 2021 had to do so alone. This made an already stressful event that much worse. And it also led to people feeling even more isolated, which affected their mental health in more ways than we can guess.

All of these factors increased the total stress people experienced. And even though the pandemic has now passed to some extent, many people have not dealt with the stress they experienced a few years back. Oftentimes, this stress has remained and turned into chronic stress, which can lead to burnout. Many people have also experienced financial stress in the past three years, as some companies have downscaled while others closed completely because of the pandemic.

Now, we find ourselves heading into a global recession, which puts everyone under even more financial strain. As you can see, the effects of the pandemic have not yet worn off, and people continue to burn out because of the acute and chronic stress they face as a result. I would go as far as to say that the mental health of the entire world has taken a dip since the start of the pandemic, leading to increased cases of burnout, depression, and other mental and physical health conditions.

Why Are the Conventional Methods Not Working?

Before getting into how to effectively cure burnout, we must consider why conventional burnout methods aren't working. If you google "how to cure burnout," you'll see dozens of articles on the topic. These articles offer advice on curing burnout and claim to be based on scientific research. Now, whether they really are based on scientific research remains to be seen. But one thing all of these articles have in common is that they focus on identifying burnout instead of curing it. This, unfortunately, is the conventional way for "curing" burnout—recognizing that you have it. But then what?

Merely identifying that you have burnout does not offer you any solutions to curing it. Of course, some websites will share information about how to treat burnout. But these methods are lacking in that they are either wholly ineffective or wholly impractical. Here are five conventional "treatments" for burnout, according to *Mind Garden* (Coultas, 2018):

Grin and Bear It

To grin and bear it after you discover that you suffer from burnout is exactly the same as what you have been doing before coming to this realization. To grin and bear it means to accept that you are burnt-out and then do nothing to treat it. It's like telling someone with the flu to just soldier on without giving them any medication to treat it or at least help them feel better. How is that a treatment plan for overcoming burnout? It isn't. To grin and bear it isn't a treatment plan; it's a fool's argument. It doesn't focus on reducing your stress load or finding a way to overcome burnout and prevent it from happening again.

Call It Quits

The other "genius" piece of advice many of these articles provide is to simply quit that which is causing your burnout. You know… quit your job, family, marriage, and life. Quit whatever is causing your burnout, and it will be cured. As you can already tell by my tone, that is not an effective cure for burnout. It's not even an effective cure for stress or any other mental health conditions. You cannot simply quit something and expect to be cured. While quitting some of your activities might lighten your burden, quitting isn't always an option, and it won't automatically cure your burnout.

Get Away From All the Stress

To "get away from it all" seems like the ideal way to overcome your burnout. You are removing yourself from that situation that is causing burnout in the first place, right? Well, that's all fine, and you will likely feel better and less stressed while lying on a beach somewhere sipping cocktails and reading your favorite book, but what happens when you return home? The causes of your stress won't simply disappear by taking a holiday. In fact, the holiday itself might even worsen your burnout, as you will now be lying on a beach worrying about all the work you have to do when you return. So, getting away from your stress is a temporary solution at best and a fast track to full-blown burnout at worst.

Figure Out What It's All About

After diagnosing yourself with burnout, many articles recommend searching for the cause of your burnout. But how is that different from discovering that you are burnt-out? And how does it help you cure your burnout? It doesn't. Yes, you should consider the factors that are causing your burnout before you can treat it. But that cannot be where your treatment plan ends. You must know what to do once you have identified the stressors in your life to successfully treat your burnout and prevent it from returning.

Set Your Mind Straight

Finally, other articles may recommend that you "set your mind right" or "change your perspective." This is just another way of telling you to grin and bear it. It doesn't offer a solution for your burnout or equip you with a treatment plan. Of course, you have to acknowledge that you are burnt-out and make treating burnout a priority before you can treat it. But simply setting your mind straight isn't an effective treatment plan.

These "treatment plans" are the primary reason why burnout statistics continue to climb yearly. Though many people have been diagnosed with chronic burnout since the start of the pandemic, few people have truly been cured of it. And fewer still know how to treat and prevent it. Most of these "treatments" are lacking in the following aspects:

- They don't involve doing less work to reduce your stress.

- They don't involve a plan to lower your expectations of yourself or work with your employer to adjust the expectations of their employees.

- They don't offer an effective solution for reducing your to-do list and, thereby, your priorities and stress levels.

As such, these "treatments" aren't treatments for burnout. But if they don't offer you the tools you need to overcome your burnout, what can?

How Do I Overcome Burnout?

If you realize that you suffer from burnout, it is time to take action. Overcoming burnout should be one of your biggest priorities. If you don't get a handle on your burnout and overcome it, it can lead to a series of other health concerns and conditions. And, as the above-mentioned "treatments" aren't effective at curing burnout, you may wonder what there is left to do.

While we will consider overcoming burnout in much more detail later in this book, you can start to ponder possible treatment plans. Once you have determined that you are burnt-out and have identified the primary areas that are causing your burnout, you can start to work on a treatment plan for it. Here is what you know about treating burnout so far:

- Identify whether I suffer from burnout using the Maslach Burnout Inventory self-test.

- Consider the areas in my life that are causing burnout. For example, do I have too many competing priorities? Am I trying to multitask too often? Did the pandemic change my income or work situation, and is it now causing additional stress?

- Consider what changes I can make to reduce my stressors and therefore treat my burnout.

By the final point, I mean sitting with a list and seeing where you can cut your schedule and responsibilities to reduce your stress. The best way to accomplish this is to sit with a list of your daily schedule— consider everything you have to do daily. Then, use a highlighter to determine which of these responsibilities you absolutely cannot shift around or drop. Once you have marked those responsibilities, you can consider which changes you can make to the rest.

For example, if picking up the kids from school or daycare takes too much time, making you late for work and therefore adding to your stress, consider whether you can ask someone else to pick them up. Or consider speaking with your employer to see if you can switch your schedule around to make time for it.

Don't remove things that help you relax and bring joy to your life from your schedule! Your daily dog walks, coffee breaks, and yoga classes aren't things you should add to the chopping block. While cutting these things from your schedule will leave you with more time, it will also reduce the number of stress-relieving activities you have.

Once you have made your list, you can work on a proactive plan to reduce the stressors in your life, free up your time, and include relaxing activities in your schedule. Only then can you work on treating your burnout and prevent it from recurring. Making time for relaxing activities, such as exercise, spending time with friends, or reading, is crucial. These activities actively reduce your stress, which helps treat your burnout. So, don't consider them as making your schedule fuller. Instead, focus on reducing the activities that add to your stress instead.

Another thing you must start including in your schedule if you wish to reduce your stress and treat your burnout is allowing for seven hours of sleep daily. Multiple studies have shown the importance of sleep in stress reduction and overall health. Therefore, if you want to treat burnout, you must give your body adequate rest.

Key Takeaways From Chapter 2:

- Competing priorities and multitasking are linked to increased burnout rates. While you may think that multitasking helps you get more done, it makes you less productive and increases stress.

- The COVID-19 pandemic has also increased stress and burnout statistics worldwide. Changes in your work environment, family structure, and income may have caused your burnout. Furthermore, the isolation many people experienced during the pandemic further increased stress, burnout, and depression.

- Conventional treatments for burnout include things like grinning and bearing it, shifting your mindset, quitting the things that are causing stress, and taking a break to destress. These treatment plans aren't effective at treating burnout or preventing it from returning.

- To treat your burnout, you must carefully consider which aspects of your life are causing too much stress. See how you can change or reduce those aspects while making time for relaxing activities and improving your sleep quality and duration. Only then can you treat burnout.

Now that you know how to recognize burnout and what could be causing it, you might consider in more detail its effect on your life. The following chapter covers precisely that topic to help you realize how important it is to treat burnout as soon as possible.

Chapter 3:

What Effect is Chronic Stress Having on My Life (Body and Mind)?

Our brains are wired to deal with stress that is intense but brief, like escaping from a predator or fleeing from a burning building. We're not wired to deal with chronic, ongoing stress, even if it is relatively mild. –Dan Lyons

Even though you now know what causes burnout and how you may have fallen prey to it, you may still wonder what the long-term effects of burnout are. Understanding how burnout affects your body and mind might help you take it more seriously. It can help you seek help faster and seriously consider curing your burnout and its effects.

While I've mentioned that burnout may lead to depression, that isn't the only problem burnout causes. Burnout can lead to several mental and physical health conditions, of which depression is merely one. In addition, chronic stress wreaks havoc on all the natural systems in your body, placing it in a constant fight-or-flight mode, which can lead to a host of other health problems.

And, as you may already know, chronic stress and burnout don't only cause physical health problems. It can also cause several mental health conditions. Therefore, understanding and overcoming burnout and chronic stress should be one of your biggest priorities. If you don't overcome it, you will soon suffer the consequences. In this chapter, you will learn what chronic stress (the cause of burnout) does to your body, the effects of fight-or-flight mode on your physical and mental health, and how chronic stress leads to burnout. This will give you a better idea of why you shouldn't underestimate the effects of chronic stress and burnout.

What Does Chronic Stress Do to Your Body?

WebMD describes burnout as the "emotional, mental, and physical reaction to constant stress" (*What to Know about Work Burnout,* 2021). As chronic stress causes an emotional, physical, and mental response, you might wonder what chronic stress does to your body in these aspects. As you learned in Chapter 1, chronic stress and burnout symptoms manifest in physical, emotional, and behavioral signs. It's fitting that chronic stress would also affect these areas of your health the most.

The Adrenal Glands and Chronic Stress

According to *Mayo Clinic* (2021), when you stress, your body alerts your adrenal glands to produce various hormones. The adrenal glands are tiny organs located above your kidneys, and they are responsible for putting you in *fight-or-flight* mode when danger, like an attacker, is near. The adrenal glands release various hormones to accomplish this state, including cortisol and adrenaline.

These hormones cause various processes to happen in the body, including an increased heart rate, mental clarity, and physical strength. By increasing your blood pressure and heart rate, you will have a short burst of increased energy with which you can flee or fight an opponent. And while these aspects are crucial for short-term stressors, like escaping a predator or fighting an attacker, they are anything but welcoming in the long run.

Chronic stress and the hormones released by the adrenal glands can wreak havoc on your body. Some effects of chronic stress include:

- poor sleep

- addiction

- obesity

- over breathing (producing too much carbon dioxide)

- fatty deposits in the arteries that may lead to heart failure, a stroke, or a heart attack

- anxiety

- high blood pressure

- depression

Another effect of chronic stress is known as *Adrenal Fatigue*. Adrenal fatigue is a condition that occurs when your adrenal glands are overworked—when they are required to produce too much adrenaline and cortisol for an extended period (Whitbourne, 2021). Suffering from adrenal fatigue may also impact your health, as your body cannot produce the hormones it needs to function correctly. Adrenal fatigue may lead to slower cognitive functioning, decreased mental clarity, and extreme mental and physical exhaustion. So, nothing good comes from feeling mentally exhausted.

While doctors have argued for many years over adrenal fatigue as a condition, more doctors now seem to recognize it as a legitimate health condition since more people suffer from chronic stress and burnout.

None of the effects of chronic stress or adrenal fatigue are pleasant and can lead to premature death. Furthermore, chronic stress severely affects your quality of life, both daily and long-term. As such, getting control of your chronic stress will help you live a healthier and possibly longer life. Because chronic stress can affect you for years to come, it's crucial to get it under control as soon as possible to minimize the damage.

Of course, your body may react differently to stress than someone else's. In addition, some people are more sensitive to the effects of chronic stress than others. Therefore, they may experience these symptoms when dealing with lower-stress situations than another person. Still, no amount of chronic stress is ever advised. Short periods of stress are okay and may lead to higher productivity, increased mental alertness, and endurance.

Considering the adrenal glands' role in instigating the fight-or-flight response you experience when severely stressed, you may wonder how this response affects burnout. What is the connection between the body's response to stress and burnout? And what are the potential risks of being in a constant fight-or-flight state on your mental and physical health?

In more detail, let's consider the link between your adrenal glands, chronic stress, and decreased mental and physical health.

A Detailed Explanation of the Body's Fight-or-Flight Response and Its Effect on Your Health

When you hear the word adrenaline, you often think of your body's "fight-or-flight response." That's because adrenaline is one of the hormones that cause this response, which makes you freeze right before jumping off a cliff or wanting to run away at the sight of a bear in your backyard. And that response is exactly what adrenaline is meant to instigate. But what happens if your body is in a constant fight-or-flight state? How does it affect your overall health?

While many healthcare practitioners and researchers argue about the reality of adrenal fatigue and its effects, nobody questions the potential harm a constant adrenaline spike can cause in your body. So, how does your body instigate the fight-or-flight response, and why is it bad to constantly have this response? The fight-or-flight response is an evolutionary ability people have developed over thousands of years of being stalked and hunted.

When you experience a sudden burst of stress, such as encountering a predator in the wild, your body reacts in a certain way. First, your brain informs your sympathetic nervous system of a threat. Then, it alerts your adrenal glands to produce more adrenaline and cortisol. These hormones increase your blood pressure and heart rate, which affects your body in various ways. For example, adrenaline reduces your response to pain and fatigue, while cortisol increases your blood pressure and your breathing. This allows for more oxygen to reach your muscles, ensuring they have the energy to fight or flee.

Your eyesight improves, your muscles strengthen, and your pain response decreases. So, when you decide to fight or flee, your body is ready for either action. The fight-or-flight response is crucial for survival, so people developed it in the first place. But, unfortunately, your body cannot distinguish between stress from external threats, like a predator, or internal threats, like being worried about a deadline or having a stressful work environment.

As such, when you experience chronic stress at work or school, your body naturally initiates the fight-or-flight response, which automatically causes these responses in your body. But being in a constant fight-or-flight state has many adverse health effects. Here are some:

The Fight-or-Flight Response Affects Your Sleep

When stressed, your mind will not shut down to allow quality sleep. Because your brain feels a threat, it will constantly remain alert, which hinders your quantity and quality of sleep. As a result, you may feel restless at night, tossing and turning for hours without falling asleep. You may also wake up to the smallest sounds, even when you aren't usually a light sleeper.

The Fight-or-Flight Response Leads to Weight Gain

The cortisol released when you are in the fight-or-flight state can cause weight gain. Gabrielle Mancella from Orlando Health (2020) explains that cortisol temporarily pauses non-essential bodily functions to put your body in an optimum fight-or-flight state. One of these non-essential responses is your metabolism. And having a slower metabolism leads to weight gain, as more energy is stored as fat.

Furthermore, when your body constantly experiences stress, it seeks quick sources of energy, like sugar and carbohydrates. Therefore, you may find yourself craving sweets and starchy foods more often when you are stressed, which can also lead to weight gain.

The Fight-or-Flight Response Leads to Anxiety

Being in a fight-or-flight state can also lead to anxiety. Since your body is waiting for action or expecting an attack, you may feel anxious or jumpy more than usual. This is the physical result of the fight-or-flight response, which shows just how bad this response is for your health in the long run.

As you can see, the body reacts in various ways to the fight-or-flight response. And while these reactions are desired in a life-or-death situation where you need to make a quick decision to save your life, they aren't desired in your everyday life. They can lead to various health conditions and may even shorten your lifespan.

Why Does the Fight-or-Flight Response Lead To Burnout?

Now that you know how stress causes the fight-or-flight response and how the fight-or-flight response affects your mental and physical health, you may still wonder how the fight-or-flight response can lead to burnout. Well, it's really simple, actually. This response is caused by stress, and chronic stress over long periods can lead to burnout.

But the fight-or-flight response can also worsen the effects of chronic stress, leading to burnout much faster. For example, if you are already stressed at work, increased feelings of anxiety, sleeplessness, and weight can only lead to more stress. And this, in turn, may decrease the time it takes you to burn out. The fight-or-flight response can also worsen the symptoms of stress or burnout, which affects your mental and physical health even more.

Given the individual effects of the stress hormones released by your adrenal glands when experiencing stress, it's easy to understand how the fight-or-flight response is linked to burnout. While it doesn't directly cause burnout, the fight-or-flight response results from increased stress, which also leads to burnout. So, when you experience symptoms of the fight-or-flight response, such as weight gain, addiction, sleeplessness, anxiety, or depression, you should consider these symptoms as a warning sign of burnout.

Of course, chronic stress that triggers the fight-or-flight response also affects your body's ability to recognize and combat fear due to a sudden and real threat. Because your body cannot distinguish between internal and external stressors, it won't trigger adequate hormones for the fight-or-flight response when you truly need them. You can see this when you experience chronic stress and try a new activity.

For example, if you first attend a boxing class, your body should produce increased adrenaline and cortisol to help you stay alert and safe during this activity. You will experience some stress when first trying a new activity, and your body will produce the correct hormones to deal with the threat of that stressor.

But if your body is constantly in a fight-or-flight state, your brain won't recognize this new threat as real. Instead of increasing energy, alertness, and strength, you will feel the same (which is usually sluggish, tired, and weak). So, chronic stress can severely affect your survival skills in an emergency, which may cost you your life if you ever face a true threat. Essentially, chronic stress conditions your body to stress—but not in a good way.

It's not like conditioning your body to a new sport like boxing. While sports conditioning will force your body to adapt and change, chronic stress will only cause your body to produce more fight-or-flight hormones, which leads to more health conditions and a lower quality of life.

Hopefully, you now understand how the fight-or-flight response is linked to burnout and why it is so important to control your stress levels, even when you experience periods of increased stress at work or school. Fortunately, there is good news. How you manage your stress can help lower your adrenal response and production of cortisol and adrenaline. As a result, you won't experience the physical and mental effects of the fight-or-flight response, and your body can effectively deal with immediate and real threats when they emerge. So, you are not powerless when dealing with chronic stress and preventing a constant fight-or-flight state.

By following the steps for reducing and preventing chronic stress and burnout, you can also reduce your body's response to regular stress and decrease the stress hormones your adrenal glands produce. As such, you can reset your brain and hormones to recognize and deal with a true threat appropriately.

Why Should You Avoid a Constant Fight-or-Flight Response?

Some people may consider a constant fight-or-flight response a positive effect. Your body is constantly prepared for action, and you can react much faster, right? Wrong! Just like training conditions your body to endure more physical strain and burns your energy reserves to supply the calories needed to complete a workout, so too does a constant fight-or-flight response condition your body not to recognize or respond to fear when it occurs.

While you will learn how to cope with chronic stress and burnout in a later chapter, I thought discussing the techniques for calming a fight-or-flight response might be helpful. These techniques can help you overcome anxiety, insomnia, and powerlessness. Verywell Mind (Purse, 2022) shares these techniques to calm the effects of a fight-or-flight response.

Monitor Your Breathing

When you feel your breathing become ragged or distressed, it's usually a sign that your fight-or-flight response is in full swing. This can make it difficult to focus or sleep, and it might make you feel highly anxious. So, when your breathing becomes shallow, focus on taking deep breaths. Breathe in for eight counts through your nose and then out for eight seconds through your mouth. This should even your breathing and calm your heartbeat, which also quickens during a fight-or-flight response.

Physical Exercise

Physical exercise has been proven to reduce stress levels and increase endorphins, also known as the happy hormone. This hormone also reduces your stress and can improve your sleep quality, assist with weight loss, and improve your mood. Physical exercise can counter many effects of the fight-or-flight response and chronic stress, which can help prevent burnout. Any exercise, including strength training, cardio, or team sports, will do just fine.

Social Support

In addition to dealing with the physical symptoms of a fight-or-flight response, you need to tackle the root cause of it. This means reaching out to someone you trust and asking for the necessary emotional support to help manage your stress and reduce the symptoms of your fight-or-flight response. Social support is as crucial for curing chronic stress and preventing burnout as managing physical symptoms.

Relaxation Exercises

You can also try managing your fight-or-flight response by reducing your stress levels, including your adrenaline and cortisol levels. Some relaxation exercises to try include meditation, yoga, and pilates. These relaxation exercises, specifically exercise and breathing techniques, combine strategies for reducing your fight-or-flight response. Relaxation exercises can also help to manage chronic stress and prevent burnout.

Using these techniques can help you manage your chronic stress, avoid and treat an overstimulated fight-or-flight response, and prevent your chances of burnout. Trying multiple techniques will offer better results and can help improve your quality of life.

Key Takeaways From Chapter 3:

- Chronic stress can wreak havoc on your mental and physical health. It often leads to obesity, anxiety, depression, insomnia, and high blood pressure. It may also cause the buildup of deposits in your arteries, leading to heart failure.

- Chronic stress also leads to a constant fight-or-flight state, which also causes various health concerns. The fight-or-flight response is an evolutionary ability people have developed to react in times of stress. However, chronic stress can also trigger this response because your body cannot distinguish between internal and external stressors.

- The fight-or-flight response causes your body to produce cortisol and adrenaline, leading to anxiety, insomnia, and weight gain, to name but a few problems. It can also increase the tempo at which you burn out.

- Fortunately, some treatments for an overactive fight-or-flight response exist. Breathing techniques, physical exercise, social support, and relaxation exercises have been proven to reduce the fight-or-flight response and, thereby, the symptoms and health conditions caused by it.

Did you know that men and women develop and handle burnout differently? Understanding these differences can help you assess your burnout and the burnout of your partner or family members. So, in the following chapter, you will learn about the difference in burnout between men and women.

Chapter 4:

Difference in Burnout Between

Men and Women

"Men are from Mars, and women are from Venus." You may have heard this saying before. And lately, people have been fighting at every corner to prove that men and women are equal in every regard. Whether you agree with this statement or not, there are some undeniable biological differences between the two sexes, including how we experience and process burnout. The two sexes experience and process burnout differently, partly because of our biology and partly because of how we are raised and society's expectations.

But several scientific studies have shown that men and women do experience burnout differently. Furthermore, we process it differently, too. While many psychologists and researchers suggested there may be differences regarding how men and women experience and cope with burnout, the COVID-19 pandemic has made it abundantly clear that they do. It's interesting to see how men and women experience and deal with burnout differently. However, it's also worrisome to think that the differences in how they experience and deal with burnout may lead to misdiagnosis and delayed treatment for either gender.

Furthermore, it's interesting to see what effect traditional gender roles have on how men and women experience and process burnout and how these gender roles fail to adapt to our modern society, causing us to resort to older norms. In this chapter, you will discover precisely how burnout affects men and women differently and what problems this may cause.

Does Burnout Differ Between Men and Women?

You may wonder if burnout differs between men and women. Some people may think it does because men and women usually process things differently—where most men tackle things from a logically-based perspective, women are biologically wired to respond from an emotionally-based perspective. On the other hand, others may argue that men and women don't experience burnout differently because a disease (as burnout is a disease or condition) manifests itself in a certain way, regardless of gender. And while that argument holds true for some conditions, many mental health conditions present differently among men and women—including burnout.

The Causes of Different Burnout Statistics Among Men and Women

When discovering how men and women experience and cope with burnout, you must consider what causes these differences. Are they purely biological, or do social norms and traditional gender roles play a part, too? Let's consider four factors affecting how men and women experience burnout differently.

Traditional Gender Roles at Home

Most research shows that women, especially working mothers, are more prone to burnout than men (Artz et al., 2021). One reason for this is that women are usually responsible for most of the caregiving roles at home. In most households, the woman is responsible for ensuring the lunches are packed, the kids are put to bed, and the homework gets done. Of course, there are exceptions to this rule, but that is a common trend, even when both parents are working.

Stereotypes Affecting Pay Increases at Work

Another factor that may cause more women to experience burnout than men is inequality at work. Many women, such as Jia, who spoke to *BBC* (Cox, 2021), don't get promoted as quickly as their male colleagues, especially if they are married and have children. While this isn't the case in all companies, many companies feel that women are less capable of handling the same workload as men because their priorities are divided between work-life and family life. And while this may be true, it makes women feel less appreciated at work, which may lead to burnout.

Imbalance of Domestic Chores and Childcare

As proof of the above-mentioned point, women are still expected to maintain many house chores, even if they work full-time. If there isn't a domestic worker, the woman is usually responsible for ensuring the house is cared for. This includes cleaning, cooking, and grocery shopping. An imbalance of domestic chores and childcare leads to burnout because a person responsible for it all has too much on their plate.

The COVID-19 Pandemic Exacerbated These Differences

Many of these differences regarding the imbalance of responsibility among men and women were exacerbated during the COVID-19 pandemic. In addition, because most people worked from home for a while, the inequality in housework, childcare, and workplace responsibilities became evident. It became clear that even in a dual-income household, the woman typically has more responsibilities within the house, which leads to an increased workload, contributing to an increased chance of burnout.

How Do These Differences Affect Burnout Statistics Among Men and Women?

As you can imagine, the abovementioned factors will ultimately affect burnout among men and women. In this case, the research suggests that most women are far likelier to experience burnout, especially if they are married or have children. The pandemic exacerbated these inequalities, leading to 860,000 women dropping out of the workforce in the USA in 2021, compared to 200,000 men (Cox, 2021). Of course, there are multiple reasons for this happening, but one cannot deny that some of these women, at least, had to quit their jobs because they were burnt-out from being overworked.

The long-term effects of these statistics are troublesome, as it leads many to doubt whether you can have it all—both a successful career woman and a mother. Many girls and women are losing their interest in being career-driven, especially if they also want to have a family. And this is causing a gender gap in the market, something society has worked for decades to prevent.

Are Men Being Overlooked When It Comes to Burnout?

While most pre-pandemic and post-pandemic research has focused on how and why women experience more burnout than men, I cannot help but wonder if we are overlooking the effect of burnout on men. While the workload at home may account for more women burning out, the pandemic certainly hasn't helped burnout statistics among men. Unfortunately, society plays a massive role in the inaccurate burnout statistics among men. Since men are traditionally thought to be stoic and distant, it is difficult to recognize when a man is merely molding to his traditional role or when he is burnt-out.

As you will see in the following section, men and women process burnout differently, which has led many to disregard burnout among men. Men are taught from a young age to "suck it up" and "be a man," which apparently means not letting your emotions show or admitting when you are overwhelmed. As you can see, traditional gender roles are one of the core reasons for increased burnout among men and women.

So, that is where we must begin when trying to overcome it. Now that you know that different genders truly do experience burnout differently, you might be interested to learn how the signs and symptoms differ between the genders.

How Do The Signs or Symptoms of Burnout Differ Between Men and Women?

Regardless of whether you believe that women are likelier to burnout or if you think that the statistics are skewed because men don't admit to burnout as easily, it is clear that there is a difference in how men and women experience burnout. And understanding these differences will help you realize when you or your partner may suffer from burnout. Men and women are known to process their emotions differently. And research has proven this by studying how men and women process trauma, depression, and anxiety. Therefore, it's only natural to assume that they will also process burnout differently.

The Results of the Maslach Burnout Self-Test Differ For Men and Women

I've mentioned the Maslach Burnout Inventory (MBI) in chapter one. This is a self-test you can do to evaluate whether you suffer from burnout or are at risk of suffering from burnout in the future. Diagnosing yourself with burnout is the first step to treating it. And as more people took the MBI test, a pattern started to develop. This pattern became clear in specific companies that used the test to determine the mental well-being of their employees. The results of the MBI test were quite interesting.

The MBI test determines your likelihood of burning out based on three categories: Inefficacy, exhaustion, and cynicism (Davis, 2014). Inefficacy relates to how productive and effective you feel at work. Exhaustion relates to how much fatigue you experience. And cynicism relates to how involved you are with your work. Having a higher cynicism score usually means you depersonalize yourself at work and distance yourself from any emotional connections.

What's interesting about the results of the MBI test is that men and women scored differently in these sections. In general, women scored highest in the exhaustion sector, followed by inefficacy. Overall, they did not feel that they felt high levels of cynicism when burnt-out. One reason for this is perhaps that women are more emotionally-based. And cynicism, therefore, seems to be an unnatural response for women, especially those with children, since they need to remain emotionally engaged at home.

On the contrary, men scored highest in the exhaustion category, followed by the cynicism category. As stoicism and bluntness are desirable qualities for men (according to traditional social bias), they find it easier to become emotionally distant when experiencing stress. Unlike women, few men reported high levels of efficacy. It seems that their burnout doesn't affect the quality of their work as much as it does among women, or so they believe.

So, regarding the signs and symptoms of burnout among men and women, you can expect that both sexes will have increased levels of exhaustion. But men will typically become more distant and withdrawn, both at work and at home. They may throw themselves into their work more, focusing on delivering quality work under the time-constraints of deadlines. They may also become cold and distant at home, failing to engage emotionally with those around them. Furthermore, they may appear disinterested in those around them, sometimes not listening to what others are saying.

Women will also have increased levels of exhaustion. They may become emotionally drained, lashing out at those around them and trying but failing to distance themselves from others. They may also start showing signs of frustration at work, mentioning how they aren't progressing like their colleagues and how they are being held back. Women are more likely to mention that they are feeling overwhelmed than men, which makes it easier to diagnose their burnout.

Effects of Men and Women Experiencing Burnout Differently

Although the symptoms of burnout differ among men and women, the effects thereof aren't too different. One study discovered that burnout causes an inflammatory response in women but not in men (Davis, 2014). This means that women are more likely to have inflammatory symptoms when experiencing burnout, such as digestive issues, aching bones and joints, and bloating. While men do not experience an inflammatory response from burnout, they do experience it from depression. But burnout can lead to several other health conditions in both men and women, as you have seen in Chapter 2.

One of the biggest problems with how men and women experience and cope with burnout is that these methods are contradictory. If both partners are burnt-out at the same time, it can lead to additional stress and tension in the relationship. Both partners will feel exhausted. And while the woman may want to discuss what is causing her stress, the man may become distant and cold toward her, even if he doesn't realize it. While the man may throw all his energy into his work, the woman may become discontent with hers and feel that she isn't making any progress.

Because men and women experience burnout differently, it is also more difficult for an employer or team leader to identify when one or more of their employees suffer from burnout. Pinpointing exactly what burnout looks like among employees can be a challenge, especially if there are employees of both genders working under you. Learning to identify the signs of burnout among both genders is crucial for helping those around you identify and counteract their burnout before it gets out of hand.

Of course, since men and women experience burnout differently, they also have different ways of coping with it. Knowing how men and women cope with burnout can help you guide your partner to overcome his or her burnout effectively.

How Do the Coping Mechanisms of Burnout Differ Between Sexes?

Considering how differently many men and women experience burnout, it should come as no surprise that the different sexes also have different ways of coping with burnout. Now, the ways in which men and women cope with burnout aren't always constructive, and they might not help to reduce the stressors causing burnout in the first place. Still, because men and women react to burnout differently, they have natural ways of coping with it, even if these ways aren't effective. But how do men and women cope with burnout?

Coping Mechanisms Men Use to Deal With Burnout

Men tend to retreat into themselves when they experience burnout. Most research suggests that most men have a harder time expressing their emotions in general. When dealing with work stress and other challenges, men tend to become even more stoic and distant. They often cope with burnout by doing things alone, such as going fishing, playing video games, or going to the gym. And while these things are certainly good for reducing stress, they aren't enough to treat burnout by themselves.

Men often shut their partners out when they are dealing with burnout. Instead of sharing their feelings and asking their partner for help, they will become emotionally distant and cold. While they don't mean to shut their partner out, it often feels that way to their partner, and their partner may start to question the stability of their relationship. This problem doesn't only occur with their partners but also with their children, other family members, friends, and colleagues.

Because men don't often feel that the quality of their work is influenced by their burnout, they also tend to throw themselves into their work—working longer hours, committing to more work, and even working over the weekends instead of spending time with their families. These methods aren't constructive and won't solve the burnout problem. However, as men are typically thought of to be the breadwinners, men often make this their priority when they feel burnt-out. This thought pattern only tends to increase the burnout and exhaustion that follows, though. It is, therefore, counter-productive for combating burnout.

Coping Mechanisms Women Use to Deal With Burnout

Women typically have an easier time sharing their emotions. When they experience burnout, they may express to their partners and loved ones that they feel stressed and overwhelmed. And although this, too, can help to reduce burnout if family and friends step in to share the load, it is now wholly effective at treating burnout. Furthermore, women may start to become overly critical of small things as they feel they are not performing as they should at work. They might start to judge everyone on the smallest of things, overreacting to some extent when things aren't done the way they like them.

For example, they might explode when the children's rooms aren't clean, when kids leave toys on the floor, or when they feel that their husbands aren't helping out around the house as they should. This behavior might affect everyone else in the house, resulting in even more stress and discontent. Women may also start to feel that they aren't appreciated at home and that the effort they put in isn't being recognized or valued. These are typical symptoms of burnout in women, and while they will externalize their feelings, they often also create more problems by doing so.

While men often make time to do things alone when coping with burnout, women don't always get the same option, especially when they have children to take care of at home. This might make them feel even more burnt-out as they cannot get a break. And as the situation progresses, women may start to feel increasingly frustrated, which may lead to a complete breakdown. Unfortunately, these breakdowns are often viewed as a sign of weakness, especially if they occur at work or in a public space. Instead of trying to understand what led to the emotional breakdown, people often judge women when this happens as being overly sensitive or emotionally unstable.

So, as you can see, neither coping mechanism works to effectively treat burnout. Fortunately, the real treatments for burnout work for men and women, regardless of how they experience or process burnout. You will learn more about treating burnout in Chapter 8. But for now, I hope you have come to realize that your partner's burnout symptoms may not resemble your own, but that doesn't mean that they aren't struggling with burnout too.

Key Takeaways From Chapter 4:

- Burnout affects men and women differently. Traditional gender roles, inequality at work, and an imbalance of chores and childcare at home lead to men and women experiencing burnout for different reasons. While most studies suggest that women are more prone to burnout, men are less likely to admit when they are burnt-out.

- Men typically experience exhaustion and cynicism when they are burnt-out. They become distant, focus on their work, and avoid emotional conversations or sharing their feelings when burnt-out.

- Women experience exhaustion and inefficacy most when they are burnt-out. They become emotional about small things, feel hopeless at work, and start to feel neglected at home when they suffer from burnout.

- Because men and women experience burnout differently, they might also experience more strain at home when both partners are burnt-out and they don't know how to deal with it or help each other.

- Men often spend time alone or retract emotionally from a relationship or their family to cope with their burnout. They find it even more difficult to share their emotions when they experience burnout and often throw themselves into their work to fulfill their role as breadwinners.

- Women often start complaining about insignificant details when they are burnt-out. They start to contemplate their effectiveness at work and often try to do too much at once to cope with burnout. Neither of these things helps combat burnout or solve the problem.

Now that you know how men and women experience and process burnout differently, you should also consider how burnout affects those around you. We often internalize all our problems when we are burnt-out, and we fail to recognize how our burnout affects those closest to us. In the following chapter, you will learn how burnout affects others at home and at work.

Chapter 5:

The Effect of Burnout on Others

By now, you already know the severe effects burnout has on your mental, emotional, and physical health. Unfortunately, burnout doesn't only affect your health and well-being. Burnout is like a bad habit, in some sense. Like smoking or drinking... While it affects the user, burnout also affects everyone around you, especially those who are closest to you, like your family, friends, and colleagues. Therefore, if you don't get your burnout under control and treated, the condition may do a lot more damage than just to yourself.

While it's normal to go through periods of stress in your life, and your family should understand that and be considerate of it, having chronic stress that leads to burnout is anything but normal. It can lead to many problems in your family and work life, and it can damage your relationships. As you've learned in the previous chapter, men and women experience and process burnout differently, so your partner may not understand why you are acting the way you are. And, if your burnout goes unchecked for too long, your behavior may strain your relationship with your children and your family.

Furthermore, despite being burnt-out from taking on too much, burnout negatively affects your productivity. Therefore, you may also encounter more problems at work if the quality and delivery of your work aren't up to scratch. Don't believe me? Let's see what the research says about how burnout affects those around you.

How Does Your Burnout Affect Those Around You?

People often assume that their stress and burnout only affect them. This is another problem with burnout; it makes you blind to the needs of others. Burnout causes you to become so self-involved and so busy internalizing your stress that you don't even realize how that stress affects the people closest to you. But it does affect those closest to you. Just like being a workaholic, burnout leads to you not being emotionally or mentally available for others when they need you. Even when you are with them, you are distant and distracted.

Eventually, burnout may lead others to lose their hope in you. They will no longer come to you if they have a problem. They will no longer trust that you are there for them. As such, unchecked burnout can potentially ruin your familial relationships and friendships. Therefore, treating your burnout as soon as possible and preventing it from affecting those you love most is crucial. How does your burnout affect your partner, you may wonder?

The Effect of Burnout on Your Partner

Burnout caused by other areas of your life may also lead to relationship burnout. Relationship burnout is often caused by chronic stress and burnout outside of the relationship. But, like other forms of burnout, it can lead to severe mental, emotional, and physical health problems for both partners and may also cause the relationship to fail. Unfortunately, if you are already burnt-out, you may not even notice that your partner is also feeling the effects of relationship burnout. Michelle Risser at *Choose Therapy* (2022) lists the following symptoms of relationship burnout:

- Frequent fighting between you and your partner.

- Feeling disengaged from them and unable to speak or connect with them.

- Feeling cynical about your partner and the future of your relationship.

- Being disinterested in having sex with your partner or spending time with them.

- Feeling that the relationship creates more stress than support.

- Daydreaming about other relationships or life outside this relationship.

- Feeling emotionally exhausted by your partner and the relationship.

- Feeling romantically interested in other people and cheating on your partner.

As you can see, relationship burnout is a very real problem, and it often causes a relationship to fail or one partner to betray the other. And although relationship burnout has similar triggers to regular burnout, its treatment differs quite a bit. Couples counseling is often needed to restore the broken trust in a relationship and allow your partner to open up to you again.

However, if you or your partner don't treat and manage your other burnout symptoms and get to the bottom of what's causing them, you won't stand a chance of fixing the broken relationship. Your burnout may lead to your partner resenting you or your job. It may cause them to feel that they can no longer depend on you or that the relationship doesn't offer the support they need. Once this trust is broken, it is extremely difficult to regain. But you cannot hope to regain it if you are still burnt-out from work.

The Effect of Burnout on Your Children

Burnout not only affects your partner. If you have children, they will also suffer because of your burnout, no matter how old they are. Children look to their parents for guidance and often model their behavior after their parents. As you can imagine, being stressed and short-tempered is not the behavior you would want your children to model, even if hard work and dedication are. When you have children, your life often becomes a lot more complicated.

You have more things to juggle and more people who require your attention. And while this may be the cause of your burnout, it's crucial that you never make your children feel as though they are the cause of your stress. Unfortunately, children will feel the effects of your burnout in the following ways:

- You no longer spend as much time with them as you used to.

- Even when you spend time with them, you are emotionally distant.

- You don't pick up on your children's needs anymore, especially their emotional needs.

- You are short-tempered and often snap at them for little things, like forgetting to pick up their toys.

- You aren't there to celebrate their achievements or watch their performances or sports games.

While these may seem minor, they can destabilize your relationship with your children. If your children feel that you aren't there for them or that they cannot come to you with their problems or fear that you will yell at them if they do, they won't open up to you. This can cause a lot of strain in the relationship and may lead to resentment on their side and regret on yours.

Therefore, treating your burnout is crucial, as not letting your children feel like they are part of the cause of your chronic stress. If you don't treat your burnout as soon as possible, it could potentially alter your relationship with your children forever. Just like with your partner, trust is a difficult bond to mend. If your children no longer trust that you are there for them when they need you, they may become distant and withdrawn.

The Effect of Burnout on Your Family and Friends

Burnout affects your family and friends much in the same way as it affects your partner and children. While they may not experience the effects of your burnout as often or as deeply as your partner and children, they may also notice changes in your behavior brought on by chronic stress. If you distance yourself from your friends and family, they might also drift away, distancing themselves from you. Furthermore, if you are short-tempered and often snap at them for no reason, they will withdraw from the friendship.

No matter how much your friends and family love you, if they feel that you are being abusive toward them (emotionally withdrawn and short-tempered), they will ultimately withdraw themselves from the relationship. Burnout often makes you more sensitive to criticism. Therefore, you are more likely to become defensive if your friends or family members mention that you may be overworked. This might create even more tension in your relationships, especially if you snap at your family for mentioning that you should take a break.

Unfortunately, if your friends and family distance themselves from you, they also distance themselves from your partner and children. This can make them feel more isolated, and they might resent you even more for this isolation. As such, it is crucial that you manage your temper when you are around friends and family. While this isn't always possible, especially when you are so burnt-out that you disengage from your emotions, it should be a priority. If you notice yourself becoming more defensive, mean, or unnecessarily harsh toward your friends and family, it might be a sign that you need to reevaluate your priorities.

As you can see, burnout affects far more people than just yourself. And while you may be so caught up in your burnout and being overwhelmed, you may not notice the toll your burnout takes on those around you. If you don't take treating your burnout seriously for your own sake, perhaps you will do so for the sake of your loved ones.

How Does Burnout Affect Your Productivity?

The irony of burnout is that you are becoming less productive in your attempt to get everything done on time. Burnout significantly affects your productivity, as does multitasking, which often goes hand-in-hand with burnout. While women are more likely to admit that they aren't as productive or efficient at work when burnt-out and men think that burnout doesn't affect the quality of their work, both sexes are significantly affected by burnout in terms of their overall productivity.

If you already feel stressed about everything you have to accomplish at work before you start your day, you will head into the day feeling negative and overwhelmed. And these feelings undoubtedly affect how you approach your tasks at work, which also affects how well and how well and how fast you complete them. Burnout affects your productivity on a personal and organizational level, as you cannot manage a team if you feel burnt-out any more than you can manage your own workload.

Furthermore, burnout not only affects your productivity at work but at home too. So, let's consider how burnout affects your productivity in various aspects of your life to help you discover just how crucial it is to treat and control your burnout and its effects.

How Burnout Affects Your Productivity at Work

As mentioned, burnout affects your productivity at work on two levels—personal and organizational. Understanding how burnout affects you on these levels at work can help you manage the symptoms and fallout of your burnout. Burnout affects your productivity on a personal level first, which then affects your company as a whole by reducing its productivity in turn. According to Laila at *Health Worker*

Burnout (2021), burnout affects your productivity on a personal level at work in the following ways:

- It creates a negative attitude toward your work.

- It causes you to become absent-minded when completing work.

- It affects your problem-solving skills.

- It causes you to lose motivation regarding the quality and quantity of your work.

- It reduces your attention span and increases your exhaustion at work.

These factors can become a severe problem at work, especially as it influences the quality and delivery of work. This can bring your job security into question, as your company will likely replace you if you are no longer a valuable asset to them. Of course, you may wonder how your burnout affects the company as a whole. Well, although one person's burnout has a limited effect on a company's performance (depending on their role in that organization, of course), the effects of burnout can be detrimental if multiple employees suffer from it. Here are a few ways in which employee burnout can affect a company's performance:

- It increases the company's turnover time leading to longer time spent on a single project.

- It leads to reduced engagement from the employees, which makes problem-solving a huge problem in the workplace.

- It affects the overall quality of work the business produces, leading to more dissatisfaction among clients and fewer contracts.

All these factors influence the company's revenue stream, which in turn affects the organization's performance and job satisfaction of the employees. As such, employee burnout can create a circular problem of decreased performance, increased job satisfaction, and a bigger workload to improve the company's profit margins, which often leads to more burnout.

How Burnout Affects Your Productivity at Home

When you feel stressed at work, you often feel less motivated to complete tasks at home, no matter how small they are. If you've had a stressful and busy week at work, you often don't want to commit to doing anything on the weekends. This leads to even the most mundane tasks, like washing, replacing the light bulbs, or mowing the lawn feels like an insurmountable task. Therefore, it's easy to see how burnout can affect your productivity at home and work.

But burnout and its consequences lead to reduced productivity at work, which becomes a bigger problem if you have a family at home. Weekends often require some effort on your part to spend time with your family, be it going to your children's sports games, going on a date with your partner, or completing the chores around the house you don't get to during the week. If you can no longer do these things because you feel too exhausted and burnt-out, your partner may feel that you are not pulling your weight at home. This may cause them to feel overworked and underappreciated and may lead to them suffering from burnout too.

Furthermore, if you don't do anything around the house on the weekends or evenings because you feel too burnt-out from work, you are setting a bad example for your children. Instead of teaching them to be responsible and take care of the things that need taking care of, you teach them that it's okay to expect your partner to deal with everything while you spend the whole day sleeping or lying around on the couch. And if you don't attend your children's sporting events or spend time with them on the weekends, they might feel neglected.

Another burnout problem is that you don't feel like engaging with others. So, instead of visiting your family, spending time with your partner and friends, or taking your children for a family outing, you prefer to stay home and do nothing to engage with anyone else. This makes others feel unappreciated and unwanted, affecting their mental well-being.

What Are the Long-Term Effects of Burnout on Others?

As you can see, burnout affects not only you and those around you but particularly your partner, children, family, and friends. And while they might be extremely understanding of your situation and support you through the difficult and stressful times at work, there will come a point where they no longer feel like a priority. As such, burnout can affect your family and friends in the long-term. You may lose some of your friends entirely if you don't make an effort to see them or then snap at them for no reason when you do.

Your partner will likely be able to endure longer than your friends. Still, your partner will also undoubtedly experience more of the brunt of your burnout, which may lead to them experiencing relationship burnout. They will start to feel unappreciated and unloved by you. Ultimately, if you don't treat your burnout, it can cause untold damage to your relationship and may lead to it failing. If your relationship endures your burnout, you will have a lot of work to do to repair the damage caused in the relationship and rebuild the trust your partner has lost.

Of course, your burnout may also lead to your children feeling abandoned by you, even if you don't physically abandon them. Because children are so impressionable and sensitive, they might experience the effects of your burnout much more personally than your friends or partner. They are more sensitive to your moods and may not recognize that you are overworked and tired. This can lead to them forming a detached relationship with you that may never be repaired, no matter how hard you try.

Finally, your burnout may bring your job security into question. If your employers, co-workers, and team leaders feel that you aren't pulling your weight at work, they might question your commitment to and ability to complete your work diligently. This may ruin your relationship with them, which may very well cost you your job.

Key Takeaways From Chapter 5:

- Burnout affects others just as much as it affects you. While you may be oblivious to the effects of burnout on others, it doesn't mean that they aren't suffering along with you.

- Your partner may experience relationship burnout due to your emotional absence from the relationship. They may lose their trust in you and feel you aren't there for them when they need you.

- Your children may also feel neglected by you and withdraw from you entirely if you don't try to be there for them when they need you (emotionally and physically).

- Your friends and other family members may feel the same. They might withdraw from the friendship or become estranged if you are short-tempered around them.

- Burnout also affects your productivity at work and at home. You feel less motivated to complete daily tasks and cynical about your work, and your problem-solving skills suffer as a result.

- Burnout can have long-term effects on others just as much as it can on you, so it is critical to treat and manage your burnout as soon as you are diagnosed with it.

Now that you understand how significant the extent of your burnout is, you may wonder how to treat and cure it. In the following chapter, you will learn why conventional methods for treating burnout aren't always effective. This might help you understand why you are not cured of your burnout even if you have been trying to treat it for a long time.

Chapter 6:

Why Are the Conventional

Methods Not Always Working?

Considering what you already know about burnout and how it works, you might still be interested to learn why so many people suffer. Surely there must be a treatment plan for burnout? And if there is, why are the burnout statistics constantly rising? Well, there are treatments for burnout. More importantly, there are methods employed by companies that try to reduce the severity and occurrence of burnout among their employees. Unfortunately, many of these treatments and prevention methods for dealing with burnout are ineffective, to say the least.

Some of them even border on being entirely counterproductive, not allowing you to combat your burnout or treat it in the least. While these methods may have shown results previously, the many people now suffering from burnout who don't experience relief by using them prove that the methods themselves are ineffective.

What Are the Conventional Methods for Dealing With Burnout, and Why Do They Fail?

Before we delve into understanding which methods people are recommended to use to combat their burnout, I would first like to explain how companies combat it. Unfortunately, many of their methods are also ineffective and merely mask the symptoms of burnout or prolong the time it takes for burnout to surface in the company. It's important to mention that some employees may find relief from these methods, and I cannot disregard them as being entirely useless. However, for the most part, they aren't as effective as employers and employees would like them to be.

Companies Offer Extra Leave for People Suffering From Burnout

Some companies offer additional leave to employees suffering from burnout. When an employer or team leader suspects that one of their employees is suffering from burnout, they might suggest that the employee take some time off from work. This leave is often called "a mental health day" or "medical leave." And while a short bit of leave, such as a day or three, might reduce your stress at that moment, it does nothing to solve the burnout you suffer from.

Providing additional leave to employees doesn't solve the problems that are causing their burnout to start with. Instead, it merely masks the symptoms of burnout and gives the employee some time to rest before returning to work and being thrown into the same stressful environment that caused the burnout in the first place. Furthermore, additional leave isn't always possible in a company, especially one crunched for deadlines at a certain time. And, since only a limited number of employees can be absent at once without affecting company performance, providing additional leave is not a viable solution when multiple employees or teams are burnt-out.

Although providing additional leave doesn't solve the problem of burnout in a company, it might help the employees feel more appreciated when offered this leave. It's a way for the organization to show they care about their employees and that they are there to support them. But, essentially, offering additional leave for burnt-out employees is merely a Band-Aid for the symptoms of burnout and fails to target the route cause.

Companies Offer Employee Support Programs Aimed at Preventing Burnout

Some companies also have employee support programs or employee wellness programs aimed at preventing burnout. These programs often allow employees to see a counselor at work who helps them deal with their burnout, chronic stress, and other problems that might affect their satisfaction at work and, therefore, the quality of their work.

Employee wellness programs are an excellent idea, and most employees who use these programs benefit greatly from them.

Unfortunately, the primary problem with employee support programs is that so few employees use them. Many employees don't know about these programs or don't know what they are about or how they can help them overcome their burnout. In addition, some employees feel ashamed to attend these programs because they feel it might negatively impact the company's opinion of them. While this is rarely the case, there have been some instances where employees have reported being discriminated against by their employers or team leads when they use employee support programs.

Many employees feel that attending an employee support program will make them appear weak and unable to manage their current workload. They also feel that if the employers were aware that they attend the employee support program, they might lose out on future promotions as the employers might fear that they cannot handle more work or responsibility. And while many employee support programs are an excellent way to deal with employee burnout, some programs also only act as a Band-Aid for the symptoms of burnout instead of targeting the root cause.

Companies Offer Incentives and Team-Building Exercises or Weekends After Deadlines

Many companies, especially newer ones, offer incentives, team-building exercises, and employee getaways for employees. Like a year-end function, these incentives and exercises are meant to reward the employees for their hard work and dedication. Some businesses have similar events throughout the year, especially after a strict deadline is met or a large project is completed. And while these incentives are an excellent way to celebrate the completion of a project and thank employees for their hard work and dedication, it is wholly ineffective at acknowledging the burnout employees may be facing.

Instead, many companies use these incentives as excuses to push their employees harder, using the excuse that they will be rewarded once the project is completed or the deadlines are met. This method can actually increase burnout rates among employees, especially if individual performance-based awards are up for grabs. In addition, this can also lead to negative competition among employees. Instead of working together to deliver the best possible work, every employee will view the other as competition and try to outwork them and win the prize.

Of course, this competition is exactly what employers want, as it drives the employees to work harder and dedicate more time to their work. While this method may yield short-term results, it is not a sustainable way to ensure the well-being of employees. Furthermore, if the organization experiences cashflow troubles, it might have to withhold the prizes and incentives, making the employees feel like they have been tricked. So, although treating employees to a nice dinner or weekend away after completing a project helps build team morale, it is not an effective way of treating or preventing burnout.

What Are the Current Strategies for Dealing With Burnout? How Do They Fail?

In addition to considering how companies are trying and failing to prevent and treat company burnout among their employees, one must also consider other methods used to treat burnout. Various people, professionals, and non-professionals use these methods to help their loved ones or patients overcome their burnout and prevent it from returning. Unfortunately, most of these burnout techniques aren't effective and fail on one or more of these four accounts:

- They don't involve doing less.

- They don't involve expecting less from the burnt-out person.

- They don't involve shrinking the to-do list.

- They treat the symptoms of burnout and not the cause.

Even though these "treatments" might make you feel better for a while, the fact that they don't encourage you to review your workload and reduce it means that they aren't effective in the long run. Instead of helping you overcome your burnout and prevent it from returning, these methods treat your burnout symptoms, which might help you feel better. Here are seven conventional methods for treating burnout and why I don't believe they are effective.

Cultivate a Sense of Purpose

One of the first problems people identify when someone is burnt-out is that they no longer feel that they have a purpose at work. As you learned in Chapter 4, one of the signs of burnout is inefficacy. So, when people see you don't feel like you add value to your company, or they suspect you might lack motivation or a sense of purpose, they often urge you to put more effort into cultivating a sense of purpose at work. This can involve making a to-do list showing you how much work you have accomplished or setting daily targets for yourself.

And while these methods may help you feel a greater sense of purpose and accomplishment at work, they don't actually help you overcome burnout. They might make you feel less overwhelmed, but that is only one symptom of burnout and not the cause of it. Of course, having a sense of purpose is crucial for delivering quality work and feeling satisfied at work, but it doesn't counter the effects of chronic stress, which leads to burnout.

Build Relationships

Another stellar piece of advice you may hear when you feel burnt-out is to work on building relationships at work. By focusing on building relationships, making friends, and getting mentors at work, you will feel less isolated and, therefore, won't feel like you are alone in your struggle. And relationship building might help prevent burnout if you can turn to your colleagues when you feel overworked. However, they might not be able to offer you any actual relief or lighten your workload. While they can offer you a shoulder to cry on, that does little to help you treat and manage your burnout.

Furthermore, building relationships at work won't help you at all if your colleagues are also burnt-out. Instead, this can cause burnout to spread like a disease within the company. Mutual feelings of discontent and being overworked will spread amongst colleagues, only making each of them feel more overwhelmed and less confident in their ability to complete their tasks successfully. As such, relationship building is an excellent skill to have at work. It just isn't effective at preventing or treating burnout in general. At least you won't feel alone in your struggle at work when your colleagues are equally burnt-out, right?

Practice Self-Compassion

People also often advise you to practice self-compassion when you feel burnt-out. Don't be so hard on yourself, and give yourself a break when you need it. Well, that's a lot easier said than done. Most people are hard on themselves at work, especially when they feel like they aren't as productive as they should be. Furthermore, if they are pressured by deadlines or project completion, they might be even harder on themselves to improve their performance. Simply telling yourself you are doing a good job won't help you feel less overwhelmed, ineffective, or exhausted.

It is, therefore, not useful advice and certainly isn't an effective method for treating burnout. That is one problem I have with many of these suggested "treatments." They only help boost your confidence or make you feel better briefly while doing nothing to target and actually treat the causes of your burnout. Furthermore, self-compassion is extremely difficult for most people to accomplish, as it is in our nature to push ourselves to improve. Self-compassion involves feeling that you are good enough at your job, which many people believe is the same as being boastful—a quality that society does not encourage.

Reframe Your Mindset

Reframing your mindset essentially means viewing things from another perspective and is meant to help with your burnout by giving you a new perspective and by helping you see things in a more positive light. However, as you already know, simply changing how you look at your circumstances is not an effective way to reduce your chronic stress and thereby treat and prevent burnout. While having a positive outlook on things and trying to look on the bright side can help improve your mood, it won't actually do anything to solve your burnout problem.

Like many of the other burnout "treatment" methods, this is just another tip to *grin and bear it*. If your stress is only temporary, such as an upcoming deadline, you may very well get through it by reframing your mindset and reminding yourself that it will all be over soon. But, as you know, burnout stems from chronic stress, which will not be cured when the deadline is met. Therefore, reframing your mindset is not an effective treatment for burnout and won't help to solve your problems at all. In fact, it might not even help reduce the symptoms of burnout.

Seek Feedback and Support

If you are feeling overwhelmed, many people may tell you to seek feedback from your employers or team leaders so they can help you determine what is causing so much stress. Furthermore, by reaching out to them for support, they can also help you overcome the hurdle that is causing you so much stress. Again, while this is an effective method for reducing temporary stressors and may help you manage your workload better by reducing your daily stress, it is not an effective treatment for burnout. By the time you are burnt-out, you are well past the point where feedback and support will reduce your chronic stress.

Many people make the mistake of thinking that burnout is merely a severe form of stress and that it can therefore be combated in the same way as stress. However, just like nervousness and chronic anxiety are two conditions requiring separate treatment plans, burnout also differs from stress. Asking for feedback and support may help with your time management and reduce your future stress, but it won't do anything to reduce or treat your burnout symptoms.

Take on New Challenges

When you feel demotivated at work, people will often tell you to try something new or to take on a new challenge. This will help you relax and take your mind off of the stress you experience at work. This is a great method for dealing with everyday stress and can truly help you feel more relaxed by increasing your dopamine levels. However, taking on a new challenge also means adding more things to your to-do list, which often isn't a possibility, especially if you suffer from chronic stress.

When combating burnout, the idea is to lighten your load and reduce the number of tasks you have to get through in a day. While a new challenge might help you feel relaxed for a while, it can also increase your stress even more as you now feel more pressure to get things done in a shorter time. Furthermore, you might start to resent the new challenge, as you constantly worry about other things while doing it, and it then turns into a burden instead of a release. Taking on a new challenge is, therefore, not an effective way of combating burnout, and it may actually do the opposite by further increasing your burnout.

Practice Mindfulness and Relaxation Techniques

Another piece of advice you will often hear being given to those who suffer from burnout is to practice relaxation techniques. Meditation, breathing, yoga, and physical exercise are all ways in which you can focus on relaxing. And these activities have been shown to reduce stress and improve your mood and energy. Being mindful means considering every action before you do it. For example, if you are invited to dinner, practice mindfulness by consulting your diary to see if you have the time for it. If not, you may resent going, as you will stress about the work you still have to complete and might not enjoy yourself.

Relaxation techniques are crucial for combating burnout. However, they aren't effective as a treatment plan by themselves. Instead, you must focus on reducing the stressors causing your burnout in addition to focusing on relaxation techniques. Only relying on these relaxation exercises to reduce your burnout may improve your symptoms, but it isn't a proactive way to treat burnout and prevent it from returning.

Many of the "treatments" discussed above are useful for managing your stress, and you should certainly incorporate them once you have treated your current burnout. Still, only focusing on these techniques isn't enough to cure your burnout.

Why Do You Sometimes Need Professional Help?

While there are methods you can try by yourself to treat your burnout, it is necessary, in some cases, to seek professional help in treating burnout. If you have been struggling with chronic stress for too long, you might feel so overwhelmed that you don't know where to start when trying to combat burnout. Some people also have a lot of difficulties reducing their workload and need help prioritizing certain tasks and reducing the time spent on others. If you are the primary caretaker at home, you may also experience increased stress outside of work, which is also something you will need help to cope with.

Therefore, it might be necessary to call in professional help. Counselors and psychologists can help you evaluate your current workload, target the tasks and areas causing chronic stress, and work with you to find ways of opening up your schedule and reducing your stress and the stressors causing it. They can also help you improve your time management skills, which are often a cause of chronic stress and burnout. Seeking professional help is the best course of action if you don't know how to approach your burnout, and burnout specialists come equipped with the tools and techniques you will need to fight your current burnout and prevent it from returning.

Seeking professional help for burnout is nothing to be ashamed of. Instead, you should be proud of yourself for recognizing that you need help and for taking the correct steps to receive it. Stress management is becoming more important by the day. Therefore, seeking professional help to manage your overall stress is also something to consider, and it might help prevent you from getting burnt-out in the future.

Key Takeaways From Chapter 6:

- Since burnout has become a bigger problem recently, many companies have taken steps to help reduce the burnout statistics in their company and to their employees. Employee wellness programs, additional leave, and incentives are some ways in which employers try to reduce employee burnout.

- Other conventional treatments for burnout include cultivating a sense of purpose, building relationships at work, practicing self-compassion, reframing your mindset, seeking feedback and support, and taking on new challenges. These methods are meant to reduce your stress and thereby overcome your burnout.

- Unfortunately, these methods don't always work, as they don't focus on reducing your workload and finding the stressors cursing burnout. Instead, they focus on managing the symptoms of burnout.

- In some cases, it might be necessary to seek professional help in dealing with your burnout. Learning how to reduce your workload, practice effective time management, and prioritize your responsibilities will help you overcome and treat your burnout.

If you don't have personal experience with burnout but realize that some of the people working beneath you or some of the people on your team are burnt-out, you may wonder how to effectively help them. In the following chapter, you will learn how to recognize burnout in your team and deal with it.

Chapter 7:

Leader of a Burned-Out Team

This book has focused on your personal burnout and the burnout of individuals until this point. But burnout doesn't only affect individuals. It also affects companies and colleagues, as you have seen in the previous chapter. This also means that you may be working with people who are burnt-out. Understanding how their burnout affects your team or company is crucial for knowing how to manage the burnt-out person and how to improve their circumstances at work to help them overcome the burnout.

Knowing how burnout affects your team and how one person's burnout can affect the productivity of your entire team will help you realize how severe this problem is and treat it as such. Having a burnt-out team isn't good for anyone, and if one person in the team is burned out, it can lead to the entire team becoming negative, overworked, and potentially burnt-out. And because the team's success is also your success, it is up to you as a leader to help the team overcome their burnout and to get you back on track.

Being a leader is about more than just calling the shots. You are responsible for the well-being of your team. And if your team doesn't perform well, neither will you. Taking care of your team and ensuring their mental and physical health is in good condition is what will set you apart from other leaders. It will also reflect on your character and leadership style, which is beneficial when you want to get promoted or noticed at work.

Furthermore, having a burnt-out team may also lead to you feeling more stress, which may also lead to you becoming burnt-out. So, to grasp the severity of having a burnt-out team, you must understand how burnout affects the productivity of your team, how to recognize burnout in your team, the causes of burnout in the workplace, and how you can promote a healthy work culture for your team.

How Does Burnout Affect the Productivity of Your Team?

When you have one burnt-out member on your team, you may wonder how their situation can affect the productivity of your team. At first, you might think that it isn't such a big problem, as there are other team members who can also take on the burden and the burnt-out team members' workload. However, you will soon realize that just one burnt-out team member can cause a host of problems in your team and may even affect the productivity of your team as a whole. If you leave one team member's burnout untreated, the burnout will spread like a disease and may cause other team members to also become burnt-out and lose their motivation for the task at hand. Understanding what causes burnout in the workplace is crucial to understanding how to treat it.

You will learn about the six causes of burnout in the workplace in another section. For now, however, it's crucial to understand how burnout can affect your team's productivity. Here are five ways in which one or more burnt-out members can affect your team's productivity.

If One Team Member is Burnt-Out, the Others Have More Work to Do

If one team member is burnt-out, it will force the others to take on his/her work. This may cause them to feel more pressure to meet deadlines and ensure everything gets done correctly. As a result, the rest of your team may start to feel overworked, which might cause the burnout to spread. Even when the remaining team members do their best to complete the work of the missing team member, they won't be able to work as fast or as diligently. This will lead to project timelines delays, affecting the team's productivity.

A Burnt-Out Team Member Can Cause an Uneven Workload for the Rest

Suppose you have two data analysts on your team, and one of them gets burnt-out and needs to take time off from work. This means the remaining data analyst will have much more work to do. While other team members may try to pitch in and help, there are some aspects of the job only a data analyst has the skills and knowledge to complete. Therefore, the data analyst may feel that they are now doing the work of two people while the rest of the team doesn't have that much more work to do. As a result, the remaining data analyst risks also becoming burnt-out, and will stall the deadline of the project, no matter how diligently they work.

A Burnt-Out Team Leads to a Higher Turnover Time

Overall, if one or more team members are burnt-out, you will have a higher turnover time. Because each individual team member's productivity is affected by burnout, the team's productivity, in general, is also affected. The burnt-out team members will take longer to complete their parts of the assignment, resulting in more time spent reaching the deadline in general. While some team members may flourish under the pressure of a tight deadline, others may not. Therefore, if they have a higher turnover time or have to wait for other team members before they can complete their part of the project, they will feel increased pressure, which can cause them to become burnt-out too.

Burnt-Out Team Members May Cause Feelings of Resentment in the Team

Another cause of decreased productivity in a team is feelings of resentment or discontent. If one person is burnt-out and needs to take some additional leave in the middle of a large project, the other team members may feel as though they are being mistreated. They might blame the burnt-out team member for increasing their pressure. As such, discontent will spread amongst the team, which will cause the remaining team members to work slower and lose their motivation to complete the project thoroughly.

A Burnt-Out Team Can Affect the Reputation of the Company

Finally, leading a burnt-out team will reflect poorly on your ability as a leader. And it will also reflect poorly on the company's reputation. Higher turnover times, decreased work quality, and decreased productivity might make clients question the organization's ability to deliver high-quality work. As a result, they might take their business elsewhere in the future, which also puts more stress on the team to source new clients. As you can see, having a burnt-out team affects your productivity in more ways than one. Therefore, you must get a hold of your team's burnout rates as soon as possible.

Recognizing Burnout in Your Team

A good leader knows how to read the needs of his team. If you pay attention to your team's well-being, you will find it is much easier to tell if one or more of them are suffering from chronic stress, which might turn to burnout if left untreated. If you don't pay attention to your team and don't take their needs and remarks seriously, you may miss it when they start to feel burnt-out, and you may notice this problem too late. Understanding how to recognize burnout in your team is crucial for dealing with it as soon as it arises. Fortunately, the symptoms of team members suffering from burnout aren't that difficult to spot, especially not when you know them well. Here are five symptoms of burnout you may recognize in your team:

Reduced Productivity

Of course, one of the first ways to spot burnout in your team is to monitor the productivity of individual team members. If you notice one of your team members suddenly starts becoming less productive, especially if they are usually extremely productive, you may take this as a sign of burnout. For example, if the team member has not experienced any personal trauma or changes, a sudden decrease in productivity is one of the first signs that they are overwhelmed and potentially burnt-out. Fortunately, if you detect reduced productivity early, you can help your team member recover from it before it leads to bigger problems.

Lack of Communication

Another indicator of burnout is a lack of communication. If you are struggling to communicate with a team member, if they aren't responding to your emails or don't listen and engage when you have a discussion with them, it might be because they are too caught up with their own thoughts and stress. Furthermore, if your team members don't communicate their needs or progress from their side, it might also indicate that they aren't focused on work, and the reason might be that they are burnt-out.

Social Isolation

While some people prefer not to mix their work lives and social lives, most people will interact with their colleagues to some extent. If one of your social team members suddenly starts isolating themselves—not joining you for lunch, declining an invitation to interact with the team outside of work, or limiting any social interactions as much as possible—it might be because they feel overwhelmed, stressed, or exhausted. These feelings may lead to burnout, so monitoring your team's social well-being is crucial.

Poor Decision-Making

When a team member is focused on their stress and cannot control their emotions at work, they might start to make poor decisions at work. This, combined with simple mistakes they don't usually make, might indicate that your team member is struggling with an emotional problem, such as burnout. If you notice a team member's decision-making or instincts are decreasing, you should consider what could be the cause. If they are burnt-out, they might be too tired and not think clearly at work. In this case, you must help them overcome their burnout so the quality of their work can also increase.

Increased Irritability and Decreased Motivation

Burnout affects not only your physical behavior but also your emotional state, as you have learned previously in this book. As such, people can become irritable when they feel chronic stress or burnout. If one of your team members is suddenly cold or distant, or if they are rude to their team members or snap at them for nothing, it is a sign that they are dealing with an emotional struggle. Exhaustion, depression, and chronic stress may cause them to act this way. These problems may lead to burnout or be the cause of it. Furthermore, if a team member suddenly loses interest in a project or doesn't seem as motivated to work as they used to, it can indicate that they are burnt-out and exhausted.

Six Causes of Burnout in the Workplace

Recognizing burnout in your team is just one half of the puzzle. The other half is determining what has caused the burnout. While the cause of burnout might not always be work-related, it often is. Understanding what might be causing burnout in your team is crucial if you wish to help your team members overcome it and increase your team's well-being and productivity. There are six common workplace burnout causes, including the following.

Being Overworked

Overworking your team will lead to many negative effects, including burnout. If your team has so much work to do that they must work late every day, are forced to work on weekends, or develop an unhealthy work-life balance, it might be time to reconsider how much work you expect them to do. If your team feels overworked, they will also feel more pressure and become exhausted from all the additional hours. This can cause them to experience burnout.

Feeling Undervalued

Another common cause of burnout is feeling undervalued. If your team members constantly do their best and you deliver high-quality results at work, they may feel discouraged when their hard work goes unnoticed. This can easily lead to feeling demotivated and losing interest in their job. It might also cause your team members to feel more pressure to do more and perform even better, leading to burnout if they don't get adequate rest.

Not Having Progression in Their Career

Stagnation is a silent killer, and if your team members feel as though their careers are stagnant, they might start developing negative feelings about work. Any additional work will feel like a punishment, which may lead to increased pressure and feelings of resentment. In turn, this can lead to chronic stress and burnout if your team members don't experience any progression at work, despite putting in more than the bare minimum. Burnout can become a real problem for someone who isn't seeing any progression, as they might convince themselves to work even harder, increasing their risk of exhaustion and burnout.

Not Having the Support of Their Team Leader or Manager

Unfortunately, many mentors don't offer their teams the support they need to perform well. Furthermore, if a team leader or manager doesn't listen to a team member's opinion on matters pertaining to their job description, they might also start to feel that they aren't being supported or taken seriously can increase their feelings of isolation, which in turn can also lead to burnout. Therefore, it's essential for a team lead or manager to consider their team members' needs and offer adequate support whenever needed.

Not Receiving Clear Communication From Their Team Leader or Manager

If a team member feels isolated or confused because their team leader or manager doesn't respond to their questions or requests, they might also start to feel an overwhelming amount of pressure. If they need the team leader's advice before making a decision that affects the quality of their work, they will start to feel isolated and stressed that they aren't making the right decision. In this case, the team member also risks becoming burnt-out, feeling isolated, and overworked.

Having Too Many Tasks Outside of Their Job Description

Finally, any person will feel an increased amount of stress if they fear that they are being misused. If your team members have too many tasks outside their job descriptions, they might feel overwhelmed, especially if they don't have adequate experience in the expected work. This might lead to them feeling more stress, which may become chronic stress or burnout if the situation isn't remedied. Therefore, it's essential to understand the strengths and weaknesses of your team to avoid overloading them with work they aren't confident about completing.

What Can Leaders Do to Promote a Healthier Work Culture?

If you know how to identify burnout in your team, and you have an idea of what is causing it, you may still wonder how you can help remedy and prevent it. Fortunately, as a team leader, you are in a position to help your team members manage their time and workload. By tracking the health and well-being of all your team members, you can ensure they don't feel overwhelmed by the pressure and can help them prevent feeling burnt-out. So, how can you, as a team leader, promote a healthier work culture that prevents burnout? Here are five methods to do so.

Set Realistic Expectations

The first way to promote a healthy work culture in your team and prevent team members from feeling overworked or burnt-out is by setting realistic expectations. Don't spread your team out too thin with multiple projects or tight deadlines. This will help your team manage their time better, resulting in higher quality work and lower turnover times. Furthermore, it will make your team feel like you value their well-being, which also helps them feel more motivated to work and reduces the chances of burnout.

Track the Time It Takes to Complete Certain Tasks and Adjust the Time Frame

Regardless of how well your team works, there are certain instances where you may fall behind schedule for reasons beyond your control. In this case, it's important to readjust the time frame for a project so your team doesn't feel increased pressure to complete the job. Furthermore, if your team takes longer to complete one part or phase of the project, extending the due date might be necessary to help other members easily complete their parts. Sometimes a tight deadline is out of your control, but give your team enough time to comfortably finish their projects when you can.

Encourage Team Members to Take Breaks

Regardless of how tight your deadline is, it is important to encourage your team members to take frequent breaks. Getting up from their desks every 90 minutes, taking an adequate lunch break, and leaving work at a reasonable hour will help them feel a greater sense of work-life balance, which easily helps prevent them from feeling overworked and burnt-out. If you have a particularly hard-working team, it might be necessary to take matters into your own hands and force them to take a break when needed.

Support Team Members Who Need a Vacation

If you suspect one of your team members is overworked and needs a longer break, encourage them to take a vacation. Vacation time is a great way for your team members to relax and escape work or home stress. While it might not be an adequate way to treat burnout, it is a better way to prevent it. If one of your team members needs a break and takes a vacation day or two, don't add to their stress by telling them how far this will put them behind. Instead, be supportive and understand that a vacation might just be what they need for their mental health.

Consider the Possibility of Remote Work

If you have a team member who doesn't function well in a stressful work environment, it might be time to consider the possibility of remote work. Having some team members work from home or rotating your team members between working from home and working in the office can also be a great way to ensure nobody feels an overwhelming amount of pressure. This is particularly useful when team members clash with each other or if one of your team members often takes on the responsibilities of others and needs time to focus on their own work.

Key Takeaways From Chapter 7:

- Understanding how a burnt-out team affects your productivity can help you realize the severity of the situation. One or more burned-out team members may result in higher turnover times, decreased motivation, and an uneven distribution of work. This can cause other team members to also feel burnt-out and may lead to an even bigger problem.

- If you know your team members well, you will find it easy to recognize when they are burnt-out. Social isolation, decreased motivation, increased irritability, and poor decision-making are some of the symptoms of a burnt-out team member.

- There are six causes of burnout for employees—being overworked, feeling underappreciated, having too much work outside their job description, unclear communication from team leaders, not feeling supported by team leaders, and not progressing in their careers.

- Fortunately, as a team leader, there is a lot you can do to prevent burnout in your team and support team members currently suffering from burnout. Being considerate of their needs, setting realistic expectations, and managing your time frame can help your team feel supported and cared for, helping prevent them from feeling burnt-out.

Now that you have all the necessary tools to deal with burnout in your team at work, you may wonder how you can overcome your own burnout. The following chapter will consider overcoming burnout and stopping it from controlling your life.

Chapter 8:

How do I Overcome This?

The previous chapters in this book should give you an excellent idea of what causes burnout, how to identify it, and help you understand its importance and effect on others so you can treat it for its serious condition. However, now that you understand burnout and how to identify it, one question remains. How do you overcome burnout? Knowing how to overcome burnout is crucial if you want to treat it and prevent it from happening again. While we will discuss prevention methods for burnout in the following chapter, this one is all about overcoming burnout.

Burnout can be a debilitating condition that affects and infects every part of your life. Diagnosing yourself or being diagnosed with burnout is crucial to determine whether you must worry about it. But now that you have determined your risk for burnout, you must consider how you will control it. Unlike other mental health conditions, there aren't any medications to prescribe for burnout (though you might be prescribed medication to treat the symptoms, such as anxiety, insomnia, and depression). Instead, you must consider the causes of burnout and configure a treatment and prevention plan based on it. Fortunately, there are several methods for helping you overcome burnout, including the use of the four R's.

Understanding the Four R's and How They Can Help You Overcome Burnout

While there are many treatment plans for burnout, you have recently learned that many of them aren't effective at treating burnout. Instead, they focus on dealing with the symptoms of burnout, or they essentially instruct you to grin and bear it until the burnout symptoms subside. Unfortunately, burnout will not disappear on its own. Instead, you must take proactive measures to overcome your burnout. Many of these measures will also help you prevent burnout once you overcome it. One effective method for overcoming burnout uses the four R's to do so. So, what are the four R's, and how can they help you overcome burnout?

Recognize That You Are Burnt-Out

The first step in overcoming burnout is recognizing that you are burnt-out. If you or one of your loved ones recognizes the symptoms of burnout and see that you display these symptoms, I would advise you to listen. You cannot hope to treat or overcome burnout if you cannot first admit that you suffer from it. Being burnt-out is nothing to be ashamed of, but you should focus on treating it. But recognizing your burnout isn't just about admitting and accepting that you are burnt-out. It is also about recognizing where in your life the burnout stems from. Three factors often contribute to burnout: habits, routines, and rituals.

How Do Habits Contribute to Burnout?

While this book has mentioned that you can adopt healthy habits to overcome and treat your burnout, it's also possible that your habits are causing your burnout in the first place. If you are in the habit of staying up late to watch videos or movies and therefore don't get enough sleep, you will feel more exhausted at work, putting you at a higher risk for burnout. If you have bad habits, like smoking or drinking, your body won't be as healthy, and you will also be at greater risk for burnout. So, while good habits can treat and prevent burnout, bad habits can cause it.

How Does Routine Contribute to Burnout?

Much like habits, routines can also be good or bad. If you are routinely a late riser, and you often have to rush to work or risk arriving late, you will feel more stressed at the start of the day. This can result in an increased level of stress throughout the day, which puts you at greater risk for burnout. Furthermore, being in the routine of not taking notes and forgetting important information can also cause more stress, increasing the chances of burnout. If you have a destructive work-life balance routine, you are also at greater risk of burnout.

How Do Rituals Contribute to Burnout?

Finally, certain rituals can also lead to burnout. If you have a ritual of going out for drinks on a Wednesday and then feel hungover, sluggish, and unproductive for the rest of the week, it might be time to change those rituals. Having a social life is crucial for being satisfied and feeling less stressed. However, I recommend taking things in moderation, especially when they affect your health and can lead to additional stress and burnout.

Of course, some circumstances are beyond your control, and breaking a habit that causes stress can be just as difficult as forming one that reduces it. But, if you recognize any of the symptoms this book discussed in Chapter 1, it might be time to pay closer attention to what is causing burnout and get a handle on it. Once you have recognized and accepted that you may suffer from burnout, you can go ahead and find a way to treat it accordingly.

Restrict the Impact Burnout Has on Your Life

The next step to overcoming burnout is to restrict its impact on your life. As you already know, burnout can wreak havoc in every part of your life. But to overcome burnout, you must try to prevent it from spilling into other areas. It may be difficult to prevent burnout from seeping into other areas of your life, but if you make this a priority, you can restrict the effect burnout has on others and can nip it in the bud before it becomes an even greater problem. There are four ways of restricting the impact burnout has on your life.

Don't Close Yourself off to Those Around You

Becoming emotionally distant from loved ones is one of the first signs of burnout. But isolation is also one of the primary causes of burnout, and feeling isolated is often caused by burnout. Therefore, if you want to avoid burnout taking a larger toll on you than it already has, you should focus on opening up to those around you, especially to your partner and children. Staying emotionally connected to them, no matter how hard it seems, will help you focus on what is good in your life. This can help you overcome burnout much easier when you have a support system in place.

Accept Help When It Is Offered

Another problem with isolating yourself from others is that it becomes even easier to feel overwhelmed when you don't have any help. But if you focus on opening up to those around you, they are able to offer you help when needed. This means that you will be in a better position to accept it. Lightening your load is one way to reduce your stress and might help you feel a bit less overwhelmed, which also helps you overcome burnout. So, don't be afraid to accept help when you need it, especially when it is offered by someone you care for and who cares for you.

Make Time for Friends and Family

If you allow burnout to separate you from your loved ones, you are allowing it to win. You also allow it to affect your relationships with friends and family, which can pose a bigger problem later. So, to prevent burnout from getting any further control of your life, you must not let it get in the way of your loved ones. Spending time with them can help you focus on the positive things in life. It can help you shift your perspective away from your busy job or tight deadlines and help you feel a greater sense of satisfaction. Being around friends and family will also distract you from the stress you are dealing with, which helps reduce the severity of your burnout.

Make Time for Yourself

Since burnout is often caused by feeling overwhelmed, you can also restrict it by making enough time for yourself. Whether you use this time to meditate, go for a run, or read a nice book, do something that makes you feel whole and that makes you happy. Sometimes you need a little quiet to disconnect from the burdens that are causing your burnout. And if that is what you need to feel better, then that is what you should do. Focusing on putting your health first is crucial for restricting the effects of burnout on your life.

Respond With an Appropriate Plan to Beat the Burnout

Recognizing and restricting the effects of burnout on your life are crucial for managing and overcoming it. But if you don't follow that with a proactive plan for combating burnout, you will never really overcome it. Instead, you will only manage the symptoms. What we're truly after here is finding a cure for burnout and beating it once and for all. Developing an appropriate plan is crucial for overcoming burnout. Your plan will be uniquely tailored to your needs and will depend on the causes of your burnout and the severity of it. Here are some ideas of what can be included in a proactive plan for overcoming burnout:

Reduce Your Schedule to Reduce Your Stress

You cannot hope to conquer chronic stress and burnout if you don't make an effort to reduce the stressors in your life. You can only do that by reducing the number of things on your to-do list. If too many responsibilities are causing your burnout, it might be time to delegate some of those responsibilities to others and allow them to help you. If you don't reduce your to-do list, you won't have time to include activities that will actively reduce your stress and help you overcome burnout.

Work With a Therapist to Target the Cause of Burnout

Sometimes, the cause of burnout is unclear, and the stressors causing the burnout come from within yourself. If that's the case, it might be necessary to see a therapist who can help you overcome your burnout by working with you to find the root cause of it. Perhaps something from your childhood has forced you to put too much pressure on yourself. Or perhaps you think that you aren't successful if you feel burnt-out. In any case, a therapist can help you sort through your past and emotions to find and overcome the cause of your burnout.

Focus On Stress-Relieving Activities

In addition to reducing your to-do list and finding the root cause of your burnout, you should also dedicate some time to stress-relieving activities. This can be whatever you find joy and peace in doing, whether it's gardening, boxing, or walking on the beach with your dog. Stress-relieving activities can help take your mind off the cause of your burnout, especially if the cause is work-related. It can also help you focus on the positive things in your life and can give you something to be excited about, which might help reduce the symptoms of burnout and improve your mood and mental health.

Learn to Say No

Many people suffer from burnout because they simply have too many responsibilities. If this is a problem you struggle with, learning to say no will be crucial for overcoming and preventing burnout. You cannot focus on overcoming burnout if you continue to take on more tasks. And while you may feel bad for saying no, especially to your employer or family, it is necessary for your mental health, and anyone will understand that. So, if you don't have time to take on another responsibility, you must learn to say no and do what is right for yourself.

Regroup Your Priorities to Cut Away the Stressors

Shortening your to-do list is often easier said than done. How do you reduce your stressors if you believe everything on your list is crucial and that you cannot simply consider cutting away some of those responsibilities? I know this can be difficult to accept and attempt, so I recommend you start with the most important points. Which factors on your to-do list are non-negotiable? For example, if your child's sports game is on your to-do list, I would reckon that is something you cannot put off. Being there for your family is crucial. Therefore, family time is something you simply cannot remove from your to-do list.

However, being on pick-up duty at school is. If you are a volunteer parent at one or more school events, it might be time to cut back on those committees and reduce your responsibilities in that area. Yes, you might upset a few people at school, but you will have more time to spend on important things, such as your job and family.

Reorganizing your to-do list and taking a long, hard look at what is on that list and which responsibilities you can and cannot shift will help you overcome your burnout immensely. Don't take on any new responsibilities if you don't have the time, and never sacrifice your relaxation or meditation time for more responsibilities. The goal of reorganizing your priorities is to identify the stressors in your life and reduce them while also giving you more time to do the things that make you happy and relaxed.

So, bear that in mind when considering your responsibilities and where to adjust them to make more time for yourself. Using the four R's can help you construct a proactive plan for dealing with your burnout and overcoming yet. While this is not a step-by-step guide as you may have expected, it is a more authentic and, therefore, more sustainable approach to overcoming burnout. Using the four R's to guide you in overcoming your burnout will give you all the necessary tools to help you on this journey and to improve your quality of life.

Key Takeaways From Chapter 8:

- There is no one-size-fits-all approach when overcoming burnout. Instead, you can use the four R's to guide you in constructing a proactive plan to beat your burnout.

- Recognizing the symptoms of burnout and which habits, routines, and rituals may be causing your burnout is the first step to treating it.

- Restricting the effects of burnout on your life is crucial for helping you overcome it and for ensuring it doesn't negatively affect those around you.

- Responding with a plan of action will give you a clear guide on how to overcome your burnout. This can include seeing a therapist, focusing on relaxation techniques, and learning to say no to more responsibilities.

- Reorganizing your schedule will help you identify your priorities and can also help you reduce the stressors that are causing your burnout.

Once you have successfully overcome your burnout, you may wonder how you can prevent it from returning. The final chapter in this book focuses on how to prevent burnout from returning to help you live a happier life.

Chapter 9:

How Do I Prevent This From Happening Again?

Given all that you have learned in this book, I believe you now have a solid idea of how to identify burnout, why treating burnout is important, and how you can treat burnout. But, like many other mental health conditions, burnout is something that can reoccur. Therefore, once you have treated and overcome your burnout, you can focus on preventing burnout from returning. Understanding that you can get burnout more than once in your life and that certain personality types are more prone to burnout is another reason why you should pay attention to the signs and symptoms of burnout.

While burnout is often neglected when discussing the topic of mental health, it is, in many ways, a serious mental health condition. Some practitioners also call it the "other global pandemic" because so many suffer from burnout—suffer in silence. And you learned in Chapter 6 that many conventional treatment plans for burnout don't work because they don't focus on targeting the root cause of burnout but instead on managing the symptoms. That is why so many people suffer from recurring burnout because it wasn't treated properly the first time.

But, by following the steps in the previous chapter, you can successfully treat your burnout. Now the task begins of ensuring it never returns. Fortunately, preventing burnout is much easier than treating it once it occurs. And many of those ineffective treatments for burnout are effective when used as a prevention method rather than a cure. So, here are seven ways to prevent burnout from reoccurring.

Prioritize Self-Care

One of the best ways to prevent burnout is to prioritize self-care. As the saying goes, "You cannot pour from an empty cup." By not putting yourself first, you won't be able to help others. If you are a leader, you won't be able to lead your team. If you are a caretaker, you won't be able to care for others as well as you should. Prioritizing self-care means putting yourself first when needed. If you don't have the time or energy to do something, you must learn how to say so. Many people consider self-care to be selfish. However, the two are quite the opposite.

Prioritizing self-care will help you care for others better. It will improve your mental and physical health, helping you to deal with stress much better. By prioritizing yourself, you are setting yourself up for success. If nobody will advocate for your mental well-being, you must do so yourself. It might be an uncomfortable discussion at times, but it will always be a necessary one. Sometimes you must learn to put yourself and your needs first. If you recognize some symptoms of burnout that you have had in the past, it is even more important to focus on yourself and prioritize your needs.

This can help prevent burnout from returning and may also help you manage your stress. If you don't prioritize yourself and your needs, you may no longer have control over the stressors that enter your life and the responsibilities you take on. So, learning to prioritize yourself and your needs is crucial if you wish to prevent burnout.

Set Boundaries

Another way to prevent burnout is to set boundaries for yourself and others. Boundaries are crucial in life; they help protect yourself and those you care for. Setting boundaries means making yourself clear. If you don't have time for additional work, you must say so from the start. If you cannot commit to working on weekends, you must make that clear to your employer. Setting boundaries and clearly identifying them will help prevent burnout by helping you manage the stressors in your life.

However, what's just as important as setting boundaries is keeping to them. If you don't enforce the boundaries when they are questioned, others will see this as a sign that you aren't serious about them. They might start pushing your boundaries more and more, asking you to do work outside of your job description or requesting that you stay late or work on the weekends even when you said that you could not. When your boundaries are overstepped, you may feel immense pressure. You might also feel like a failure as you couldn't step up for yourself when needed. These feelings can increase your chances of burnout.

But setting boundaries doesn't merely apply to others. No, you must also set boundaries for yourself. These can be especially important if you work from home or have a Type A personality. Being a workaholic isn't a good quality, and it may lead to feeling overwhelmed and burnt-out. So, if you know what behavior causes your burnout, you must set boundaries for yourself to prevent you from resorting to that behavior and potentially burning out again.

Practice Mindfulness

Practicing mindfulness is another way to prevent burnout. If you know that you are stressed at work, avoiding stressors at home, such as large family gatherings or arguments with your partner, can help you feel more relaxed. While you cannot always control the stressors at home, you can communicate your feelings with your family, which might help them understand your situation and show more consideration toward your needs.

Furthermore, being mindful of your actions can help you feel more relaxed. Mindfulness doesn't only relate to watching out for stressors in your life. It also means considering which projects you take on and how much time you will need to complete certain tasks. For example, if you have a deadline coming up for one project, you may have to decline certain social invitations to ensure you have enough time to focus on your work without feeling too much pressure. Being mindful means making life easier for yourself so you don't increase the pressure you put on yourself.

Keeping a journal to track all your assignments and obligations, focusing on time management, and ensuring you eat healthily and get enough sleep are some ways to be mindful when feeling increased stress. These small actions might help decrease your stress and help you avoid recurring burnout. Being mindful also means monitoring your emotions and feelings and acting as soon as you realize that you may be heading for another burnout episode.

Take Breaks

Feeling overworked and exhausted are some of the first signs of burnout and can lead to severe burnout if these feelings aren't managed. Fortunately, you can avoid burnout by taking small breaks whenever needed. Taking small breaks throughout your working day, such as every 90 minutes, and longer breaks on the weekends can help manage your stress levels and may reduce the likelihood of another burnout episode. If the small breaks you take at work and the longer ones you take on the weekend don't reduce your stress, it might be necessary to take an even longer break.

Fortunately, companies offer sick days; some even have mental health days you can take when you feel overworked. Taking a break when needed helps you to manage your stress and can also help you identify the signs of burnout before they occur. Nobody can work 24/7; if you do, your body will force you to take a break sooner or later. Therefore, it's crucial that you give your body (and your mind) the time it needs to rest.

If you have an upcoming deadline at work and cannot take a break when you need to, you must communicate your feelings with your team lead or manager so they know what is happening. Then, you can arrange for a vacation day once the project has been completed so you can focus on getting the rest you need and feeling recovered from the recent stress you faced.

Practice Time Management

Time management is crucial for preventing stress and burnout. If you don't know how to manage your time, you will find that you have too much work to do and too little time to do it. This can cause you to feel increased pressure to deliver on your projects, making you feel overworked and burnt-out. Therefore, if you know that time management is something you struggle with, now is the time to be mindful and focus more on improving your time management skills. There are many ways to improve your time management, such as:

- Using a time management app to help you plan your day.

- Noting down all your projects or tasks in a journal to help you track your day.

- Not scheduling too many things at once.

- Ensuring that your schedule allows for last-minute changes.

Of course, there are times when even the best time management is not enough to keep you on track, especially when someone else causes you to fall behind with work and other responsibilities. But that does not mean you shouldn't still try to manage your time as effectively as possible. And time management is about more than just writing everything you have to do down. Time management means sticking to the schedule you have created.

Too many people have beautiful journals and useful online time management apps that lay discarded on their desks. If you do not use the resources at your disposal, your time management skills may not be as good as they should be. This can lead to increased pressure which may also cause burnout.

Seek Support

If you feel overwhelmed and suspect it might lead to burnout if you don't address these feelings soon, you should seek support immediately. Your friends, family, and colleagues can help lighten your load and reduce your stress if you ask them to. You can also see a therapist to help you manage your time better and prioritize what is truly important. Seeking support and asking for help is not a sign of weakness. Instead, it is a sign of maturity and inner strength. Knowing when to ask for help is crucial in times of stress and can help prevent burnout.

While you should turn to others when you feel stressed or overwhelmed, you should also recognize that they might be unable to offer you the support you seek. Therefore, it's important to clearly communicate your needs with those who offer support and explain how they can help you. Failing to communicate your needs might confuse others and make you feel even more frustrated. This can increase your chances of feeling burnt-out, as your frustration leads to more stress.

Another important thing to remember is that others may also recognize your burnout symptoms before you do. If your partner, children, or close friends approach you and offer their help to lighten your burden, it is always a good idea to accept their help. They might see that you are struggling to get through everything that is expected of you, and they might want to help you whether you ask them or not. If someone offers their help in this case, it will be in your best interest to accept it and to tell them what they can do to help. Seeking support and accepting other people's help will reduce your stress and thereby help reduce your chances of getting burnt-out again.

Create a Positive Work Environment

Yet another way to prevent burnout, especially if your burnout stems from a stressful environment, is to create a more positive work environment. Whether you are a team leader or manager at work or merely an employee, your approach to conflict at work and stress management can help you and others feel more positive about their work environment. Being a supportive coworker and getting to know your colleagues can help you bond with them. This will make you feel less isolated and more inclined to ask for help when needed.

Being in a positive work environment also reduces your stress, as work won't feel like a punishment and instead like a joy. If you are satisfied with your work, you won't feel as negative when times are stressful. However, if you don't have any job satisfaction, or if you work in a toxic environment that only increases your stress levels, it might be time to consider another line of work or move to another company. While your job is important, and you cannot survive without working and making an earning, you also cannot work in an environment that is killing you.

If you are in a management position at work, it is up to you to ensure that your team and the other employees at your job also have a positive work experience. Taking your team out for a celebration after a deadline is met, making the time to listen to their needs and input, and recognizing the signs of burnout in your team can also help you detect burnout in the workplace before it becomes a problem. This will not only help your employees, but it will also prevent you from feeling increased pressure which might turn into burnout.

Using these seven tips can help you prevent burnout and lead a more satisfying life. If you make a conscious effort to reduce your stress and manage it when it arises, you will have a better grip on your emotions, won't feel as depleted and overwhelmed, and won't fall prey to burnout as easily.

Key Takeaways From Chapter 9:

- Knowing how to treat and overcome burnout is important. But knowing how to prevent it is equally important. If you cannot prevent burnout when you feel it is approaching, you may suffer from it time and again.

- There are seven methods to reduce your stress: prioritize self-care, set boundaries, practice mindfulness, take breaks, practice time management, seek support, and create a positive work environment.

- By using these methods to prevent burnout, you can stop burnout in its tracks. It will also help you recognize burnout in others, making it easier to help them through it too.

Congratulations! You now know everything one should know about burnout, recognizing it, and managing it. The only thing left to do is to utilize what you have learned in this book and reduce your stressors to overcome your burnout. With the right tools, like the ones you now have, you can overcome and prevent your burnout, and you can live a happier life with a normal amount of healthy stress.

Conclusion

Burnout is a silent killer in our society. It creeps in from the shadows and is on you before you know it. Many people find it difficult to recognize that they are burnt-out or to admit it when they are. Many feel that the immense stress they experience is just a part of life and that they will overcome it if they work harder. But, as you know after reading this book, burnout stress is not the type of stress that just goes away on its own. Burnout is a condition, and just like many other conditions, it needs a treatment plan and takes time to treat and overcome.

In the first chapter of this book, you learned exactly what burnout is and how it is caused. You learned that certain personality types are more vulnerable to the effects of burnout and that certain habits and lifestyle choices also increase your chances of burning out. You learned the signs and symptoms of burnout and how to use the Maslach Burnout Inventory self-test (in the appendix below) to help you determine if you are burnt-out.

Chapter 2 focused on establishing what caused your burnout. Conflicting priorities, trying to multitask, and taking on too many responsibilities often lead to burnout. The COVID-19 pandemic has also had an immense effect on people and has caused burnout statistics to skyrocket. The chapter also briefly discussed how to overcome and prevent burnout and why conventional treatment methods aren't working to overcome burnout effectively.

In Chapter 3, you learned about the effects of chronic stress, which causes burnout, on your mental and physical health. Chronic stress causes many health conditions and might lead to premature death. Chapter 4 focused on the differences between how men and women experience and cope with burnout. While some research suggests that women are at greater risk of burnout, other research argues that men are often undiagnosed with burnout.

Chapter 5 taught you about the effects of burnout on others. Burnout not only affects you but also those around you. Your partner, children, family, friends, and coworkers may suffer alongside you if you are burnt-out. Therefore, overcoming your burnout is even more important than you initially thought. Chapter 6 explored in greater detail why conventional burnout treatment methods don't work. Most of these methods have a grin and bear it approach. They aren't effective at truly treating burnout, and they instead focus on treating the symptoms, leaving the root cause untouched.

In Chapter 7, you learned about your role as a leader when your team is burnt-out. You learned how burnout affects productivity in your team, what can cause burnout at work, and how you, as a manager, can help your employees reduce their burnout and overcome it. Chapter 8 and Chapter 9 explored how to overcome and prevent burnout to stop it from controlling your life. Using the methods and tips discussed in these chapters will help you overcome burnout and stop it from happening again.

I know that burnout can make you feel overwhelmed and might convince you that there is no way to escape it. However, if you calm your mind and focus on using the methods discussed in this book, you can surely overcome your burnout and prevent it from ever happening again. You can also easily recognize burnout in others, such as your children, partner, friends, and coworkers. And you can help them overcome it too. Burnout doesn't have to be a life sentence. And if the treatments you have followed until now haven't delivered lasting results, perhaps it is time you seek another treatment plan.

Remember that there is no instant cure for burnout. Employing the methods discussed in this book will help you overcome burnout, but it will take time. There also isn't a one-size-fits-all cure for burnout. Therefore, it is up to you to determine which methods work and which don't. But you now have all the necessary tools to see it through and help you overcome and prevent burnout. Whether you have dealt with chronic stress for many years or it is a side effect of the pandemic, I am pleased to tell you that you no longer have to allow stress to control your life. Take charge of your own future and manage your stress.

Thank you for reading my book! It brings me immense joy to know that I have helped others overcome a problem I have faced myself. And it would bring me even greater joy if you could review this book. Sharing your thoughts and opinions helps me get to know my readers better and makes it easier to consider what you need and want from future books. I wish you the best of luck on your journey to overcoming burnout and hope you never have to experience it again.

Appendix:

The Maslach Burnout Inventory

Self-Test

Disclaimer: The following Maslach Burnout Inventory assessment is based on an MBI assessment provided by HealthLinks (healthinks.org)

This is the Maslach Burnout Inventory Self-Test, a test produced to determine whether you are at risk for suffering from burnout or if you possibly already are burnt-out. I recommend taking this self-test at the start of the book to see how great your chances of burnout are and to act accordingly. Using this test as a guideline to determine your risk for burnout can help you determine the cause of it and act fast to reduce your chances of burnout, treat your current burnout, and prevent burnout from returning.

However, it's important to note that the MBI test is not meant to serve as a complete diagnosis of burnout. Only a trained professional can do this. But the burnout test can be used to determine your risk for burnout and may help you treat it swiftly.

The following questions are meant to determine if you are burnt-out or at a higher risk of suffering from burnout. For each of the 22 questions, decide how frequently you experience these symptoms and use the scoring system below to see how great your risk for burnout is. The scoring system for the MBI test works as follows:

0 - never

1 - a few times yearly

2 - once a month or more

3 - several times monthly

4 - weekly

5 - several times weekly

6 - daily

Section A: Occupational Exhaustion

Questions for Section A	0	1	2	3	4	5	6
I feel overwhelmed by my work.							
Working with people all day is exhausting.							
It requires a lot of effort to work directly with people.							
I feel like I am at a breaking point with my work.							
My work frustrates me.							
I feel exhausted from my work.							
I feel that I work too hard.							
Total for Section A							

Section B: Depersonalization

Questions for Section B	0	1	2	3	4	5	6
I feel tired when I wake up and think about work.							
I fear that my job is making me cold at work.							
My work makes me insensitive to others.							
I don't really care what happens to my clients or how they feel.							
My patience is at an end when the workday is done.							
I consider my clients more as objects than people.							
My clients make me feel like I am responsible for their problems.							
Total for Section B							

Section C: Efficacy

Questions for Section C	0	1	2	3	4	5	6
I effectively care for my clients' needs.							
I feel that I have a positive influence on others through my work.							
I find it easy to create a relaxing environment for my clients.							
I feel energized when working with clients at work.							
I feel energized at work.							
I feel like my work is worth something.							
I can handle emotional problems at work with calmness.							
I easily understand and empathize with my clients.							
Total for Section C							

How to Interpret the Scoring Results for the MBI Test

Once you have completed the MBI test, you can evaluate the results to determine if you are at greater risk for developing burnout. Sections A and B have a score of 42, while Section C has a score of 48. The higher you score in each section, the more likely you are burnt-out or heading for burnout. Of course, scoring higher in one section and not so high in the other two doesn't mean that you are less likely to experience burnout.

If you scored lower than 17 for Section A, you have a low to moderate chance of burnout due to occupational exhaustion. If you score between 18 and 29 for Section A, you have a moderate risk for burnout because of occupational exhaustion. If you score above 30 for Section A, you are at high risk for burnout because of occupational exhaustion. While scoring low to moderate for Section A does not mean you don't suffer from burnout. Instead, it merely means that you don't experience occupational exhaustion quite as much.

If you scored lower than five for Section B, you have a lower level of depersonalization at work, putting you at a lower risk for burnout. If you scored between six and eleven for depersonalization in the MBI test, you have a moderate level of depersonalization at work, which means you have a slightly higher risk for burnout because of it. Finally, if you scored above 12 for depersonalization, you are at a higher risk of burnout because of it.

If you scored lower than 33 for efficacy, you are at high risk for burnout. It means that you don't find any job satisfaction, which is one of the leading causes of burnout at work. If you scored between 34 and 39 for efficacy, you are at moderate risk for burnout because of it. If you scored above 40 for efficacy, you likely feel accomplished at work and are far less likely to burn out because of it.

Using the MBI test and these results can help you determine the root cause of your burnout, which you can then treat and reduce by using the advice shared in this book. Determining your risk for burnout is a crucial first step for treating and preventing it, and the MBI self-test is a proven way of showing you how likely you are to burn out.

References

Abramson, A. (2021, October 1). *The impact of parental burnout.* Apa. https://www.apa.org/monitor/2021/10/cover-parental-burnout

Abramson, A. (2022, January 1). *Burnout and stress are everywhere.* American Psychological Association. https://www.apa.org/monitor/2022/01/special-burnout-stress

Angelini, G. (2023). *Big five model personality traits and job burnout: a systematic literature review.* BMC Psychology, 11(1). https://doi.org/10.1186/s40359-023-01056-y

Artz, B., Kaya, I., & Kaya, O. (2021). *Gender role perspectives and job burnout.* Review of Economics of the Household, 1–24. https://doi.org/10.1007/s11150-021-09579-2

Brearley, B. (2020, June 6). *Too Many Priorities: What to Do When You're Asked to Do It All.* Thoughtful Leader. https://www.thoughtfulleader.com/too-many-priorities/

Brooks, C. (2022, September 1). *Why You Need to Worry About Employee Burnout.* Business. https://www.business.com/articles/why-you-need-to-worry-about-burnout/

Burn-out an "occupational phenomenon": International Classification of Diseases. (2019, May 28). World Health Organization. https://www.who.int/news/item/28-05-2019-burn-out-an-occupational-phenomenon-international-classification-of-diseases

Burnout. (2019). Psychology Today. https://www.psychologytoday.com/za/basics/burnout

Burnout Self-Test Maslach Burnout Inventory (MBI). (n.d.). https://mondiahealth.co.za/wp-content/uploads/2021/06/Maslach-Burnout-Inventory-MBI.pdf

Mayo Clinic. (2021, July 8). *Chronic Stress Puts Your Health at Risk.* Mayo Clinic; Mayo Foundation for Medical Education and Research.https://www.mayoclinic.org/healthy-lifestyle/stress-management/in-depth/stress/art-20046037

Comer, J. (2022, March 17). *The Fallacy of Multitasking.* Psychology Today. https://www.psychologytoday.com/za/blog/beyond-stress-and-burnout/202203/the-fallacy-multitasking

Coultas, I. (2018, May 21). *5 Traditional Approaches to Burnout.* Mindgarden. https://www.mindgarden.com/blog/post/36-5-traditional-approaches-to-burnout

Cox, J. (2021, October 4). *Why women are more burned out than men.* BBC. https://www.bbc.com/worklife/article/20210928-why-women-are-more-burned-out-than-men

Davis, P. (2014, April 29). *How Burnout Impacts Men & Women Differently.* Psychology Today. https://www.psychologytoday.com/intl/blog/pressure-proof/201404/how-burnout-impacts-men-women-differently

Dreme Mclennon, H. (2019, June 6). *Overcoming Burnout: 4 Rs of Self Care.* Healing Arts Counseling Center. https://healingartscounselingcenter.com/4-rs-of-self-care/

Employee Burnout: Causes, Symptoms and How to Prevent It. (n.d.). Nectarhr.com. https://nectarhr.com/blog/employee-burnout

Fight or Flight Response. (2022). Psychology Tools. https://www.psychologytools.com/resource/fight-or-flight-response

How Parental Burnout is Affecting Moms, Dads, and Caregivers. (n.d.). Willowstone Family Services. https://www.willowstone.org/news/parental-burnout

How To Prevent Employee Burnout & Maximize Productivity. (n.d.). GrowthForce. https://www.growthforce.com/blog/how-to-prevent-employee-burnout-maximize-productivity

How to Recover from Burnout, the 4R's. (n.d.). Burned out Business Mom. https://www.theburnedoutbusinessmom.com/blog/deal-with-burnout-with-this-4-step-system

Johnson-Greene, C. (2018, December 13). *Burnout Symptoms Can Affect Both Your Career and Family Life.* University Health News. https://universityhealthnews.com/daily/stress-anxiety/burnout-symptoms-can-affect-career-family-life/

Kato, B. (2021, December 28). *The real reason why women burn out faster than men.* New York Post. https://nypost.com/2021/12/28/the-real-reason-why-women-burnout-faster-than-men/

Laila. (2021, May 3). *How Does Burnout Affect Productivity?* Health Worker Burnout. https://healthworkerburnout.com/how-does-burnout-affect-productivity/

Lluch-Sanz, C., Galiana, L., Doménech-Vañó, P., & Sansó, N. (2022). *The Impact of the COVID-19 Pandemic on Burnout, Compassion Fatigue, and Compassion Satisfaction in Healthcare Personnel: A Systematic Review of the Literature Published during the First Year of the Pandemic.* Healthcare, 10(2), 364. https://doi.org/10.3390/healthcare10020364

Malesic, J. (2022, January 4). *Opinion | How Men Burn Out.* The New York Times. https://www.nytimes.com/2022/01/04/opinion/burnout-men-signs.html

Mancella, G. (2020, February 12). *How too much stress can cause weight gain (and what to do about it).* Orlando Health.

https://www.orlandohealth.com/content-hub/how-too-much-stress-can-cause-weight-gain-and-what-to-do-about-it

Murray, D. (2021, August 18). *10 Jobs With The Highest Burnout Rates (and 5 of the Lowest)*. Slice. https://www.slice.ca/jobs-with-the-highest-and-lowest-burnout-rates/

Purse, M. (2019). *Understanding and Treating Acute Stress (Fight or Flight) Response.* Verywell Mind. https://www.verywellmind.com/taming-the-fight-or-flight-response-378676

Risser, M. (2022, August 2). *Relationship Burnout: Signs, Causes & How to Overcome.* Choosing Therapy. https://www.choosingtherapy.com/relationship-burnout/

Salvagioni, D. A. J., Melanda, F. N., Mesas, A. E., González, A. D., Gabani, F. L., & Andrade, S. M. de. (2017). *Physical, psychological and occupational consequences of job burnout: A systematic review of prospective studies.* PLOS ONE, 12(10), e0185781. https://doi.org/10.1371/journal.pone.0185781

Saunders, E. (2019, July 5). *6 Causes of Burnout, and How to Avoid Them.* Harvard Business Review. https://hbr.org/2019/07/6-causes-of-burnout-and-how-to-avoid-them

Scott, E. (2006, June 12). *What It Means to Have Type A Personality Traits.* Verywell Mind. https://www.verywellmind.com/type-a-personality-traits-3145240

Scott, E. (2022, October 16). *How to Tell You Have Reached the Point of Burnout.* Verywell Mind. https://www.verywellmind.com/stress-and-burnout-symptoms-and-causes

Signs you might be experiencing a burnout and how to regain balance in your life. (2021, November 22). Darling Downs Health. https://www.darlingdowns.health.qld.gov.au/about-us/our-stories/feature-articles/signs-you-might-be-experiencing-a-burnout-and-how-to-regain-balance-in-your-life

Smith, M., Segal, J., & Robinson, L. (2018). *Burnout prevention and treatment.* HelpGuide https://www.helpguide.org/articles/stress/burnout-prevention-and-recovery.htm

Sutton, J. (2022, January 9). *The Fight-or-Flight Response: Everything You Need to Know.* PositivePsychology.com. https://positivepsychology.com/fight-or-flight-response/

Weber, A. (2021, February 18). *The Real Reasons Why We're Not Curing Burnout.* TLNT. https://www.tlnt.com/the-real-reasons-why-were-not-curing-burnout/

What to Know About Work Burnout. (2021, October 5). WebMD. https://www.webmd.com/mental-health/what-to-know-about-work-burnout

Whitbourne, K. (2021, February 27). *Adrenal Fatigue: Is It Real?* WebMD. https://www.webmd.com/a-to-z-guides/adrenal-fatigue-is-it-real

Wilding, M. (2022, August 22). *3 Types of Burnout, and How to Overcome Them.* Harvard Business Review. https://hbr.org/2022/08/3-types-of-burnout-and-how-to-overcome-them